The essays in this book appeared
between April 1994 and November 1995 in the *St. Paul Pioneer Press,*
which has granted permission to reprint them.

**Library of Congress Catalog Card Number: 96-94034**
Second printing 1998
First printing 1996
ISBN 0-9651137-0-1

Published by
Melpomene Institute
1010 University Avenue
St. Paul, Minnesota 55104

# OF HEROES, HOPES & LEVEL PLAYING FIELDS

*A Collection of Insights and Observations*
*on Physical Activity and Women*

**JUDY MAHLE LUTTER**

**MELPOMENE INSTITUTE**

# Contents

## Level Playing Fields

# *Foreword*

Yesterday I left work early to go "bouldering" with a friend at Stoney Point, a local climbing spot near my home in the San Fernando Valley area of Los Angeles. My friend and I recently started climbing together on weekends and have begun scheduling the mid-week 4:00 P.M. "rock time" to practice our climbing skills, much like those who take off for afternoon "tee time." Even after three afternoons of this, I still haven't gotten used to leaving work before dark and not returning.

After exchanging initial greetings yesterday, neither my climbing partner nor I were our typical "up" selves. We'd both had gray days. However, getting lost in climbing for an hour fixed that. We both talked about how much better we felt afterwards.

One of the themes of this book is taking time for yourself to enjoy the benefits of being physically active. The book is full of heroic stories and victories to which we can all relate. While I struggle with leaving work for some afternoon recreation, a single and sole bread-winning mom must wrestle not only with her schedule but with her choice. Can she justify taking the time for physical activity?

Author Judy Lutter tells how one such single mom makes the time for regular afternoon walks by doubling up, pulling her children in a wagon behind her while she reviews her notes for a class she is taking. This woman realizes that she is teaching her children about taking time for their own well-being.

This book is rich in lessons not just about physical activity but also about living fully, realizing our capabilities. Many of

Judy's heroes are also mine, like Linda Bunker, a dean at the University of Virginia and noted scholar in sports psychology. Having known Linda for years, I've always found her spirit to be as exceptional as her mind. This is even more evident now as she continues to teach and lecture at the same time as she battles with cancer. Her story redefines life's limits. Linda teaches us to expand from them, to go forward focusing on what we can do rather than dwelling on what we have lost.

Again and again, author Judy Lutter reflects her own brilliance of mind and spirit by the stories she has chosen and the details that she notes. By doing so she reveals her own character. While I've had the privilege of knowing Linda Bunker's story, many of you have not. Thanks to Judy, many more of you will know now.

Another hero in this book is Joan Benoit Samuelson. Most of us know Joan as the first woman to win the Olympic Marathon. How many of us know the gold that is inside Joan? Or her quest for balance? Or that now she uses her watch to know when to pick up her kids rather than to time her splits. While Joan is currently set to compete for a slot on her second Olympic team, she no longer risks everything for it. Her true heroism lies in her willingness to walk away from fame to her children and other priorities. And finding peace in those choices.

The best gift we can give ourselves is to live life fully throughout our time on earth. It means having the courage to face challenges, such as taking up running for the first time at age sixty-nine. Whatever we do, we all need heroes and we need hope to spur us on. Judy has given both to us in this book and much for a legacy that we can give to young girls. Having heroes and hope, we can mentor them to know there are no limits. All we need to say is simply, "Look at me." I hope I'll be climbing when they are looking.

— *Barbara Harris*
*Editor in Chief,* SHAPE *Magazine*

# Introduction

When I was a kid, I had no idea I would end up being who I am or doing what I do. It never occurred to me that I would become a competitive athlete or found and direct an organization concerned with physical activity and health. The fact that these have come to be true says as much about changes in society as in me.

As a growing child, I could have used the self-esteem we now know sports provide for girls. I'd been physically active as a young child — playing with the neighbor boys in the alley — but by the time I turned ten, the boys were saying, "We don't play with girls." This shocked me, even more so because the same thing was happening at school. By fourth grade, recess was no longer co-ed: the boys played baseball, while the girls skipped rope or gossiped.

I was a fat kid who lost self-confidence in fourth grade. To compensate for the hurt of feeling that I didn't belong, I retreated to books. In high school, I participated in the Girls Athletic Association (GAA) — my generation's answer to intramural sports — but I was never very good and I knew it.

The turning point came when I was thirty-three. One night, tired and frustrated by a day at home with my three young children, I announced I was going on a run.

As I went down my front steps, I prayed I could make it as far as the corner. I did manage to run that first two hundred feet. I was glad, because as I glanced back I saw my family watching, noses pressed to the window. As soon as I was out of sight, though, I walked. I tried to run a bit every once in a while, but there was no way I could run consistently. Even so, by the time I came back home I was more relaxed.

When I returned, the kids were in bed. Their dad had read them their story; the house was calm and quiet. Even though my legs hurt the next morning, I decided to try running again that night. I discovered I could run a little bit farther. I relished the fact that I was getting out of the house, alone. Within a week I realized I would feel better if I went running every night.

When I started running, I was beginning to understand that I needed more time to myself. My husband, Hap, and I then began to make changes so that I could have more unstructured time. Running out the door became the invitation for me to explore what I wanted to do and become in the years ahead.

I discovered I was a good runner. At my first athletic competition, people cheered as I crossed the finish line. I felt something I'd never experienced before: a new sense of competence and independence.

To my surprise, women began calling to ask questions about physical activity and their health. They thought I might have answers because I was conducting research on women at the University of Minnesota. When I couldn't find answers, I became curious. Why was there so little information about girls and women? I thought perhaps I should try to discover some of the answers myself.

Hap and my running friends encouraged me. With their help, I co-founded Melpomene Institute for Women's Health Research, in 1982. Since then, Melpomene has explored the link between physical activity and health for girls and women of all ages. My work has given me the chance to listen to many voices, to do research in a number of arenas, to speak to audiences nationwide and to write.

In 1993, I began to discuss the idea of a weekly column with the editors of the *St. Paul Pioneer Press,* St. Paul, Minnesota's daily newspaper. Because the scope of Melpomene's interests is broad, we discussed placement in the lifestyle section as well as in the sports section. The newspaper staff decided to place it on the Sunday sports pages.

My feelings about the choice were mixed. I sympathized with many of my female friends who skipped the sports section. They felt that reading it was a waste of time because most of the news was about professional male sports. Yet I was among the first to applaud as girls and women received greater coverage, and I believe it's important for women to support the changes that are being made. There is far greater coverage of amateur, women's and girls' activities now, and we need to praise the editors when coverage is good.

Women also need to let the editors of sports pages know that we are among their readers. Woman are still a very small minority on the sports pages, but we do belong there, in the same way as we belong on sports teams and engaging in any sort of physical activity we choose. More and more of us are finding that physical activity is important to our self-definition. I continue to find the opportunity and the time to dream on my daily run. I know I am less stressed and more fun because I have found this means of joyful expression. I'm dedicated to helping more girls and women add this kind of richness to their lives.

In my two years of writing for the newspaper, I've learned a lot, made some changes and accepted some limitations. My editors have given me great support as well as leeway in my range of topics. I've interviewed interesting people and discovered issues and sports that were entirely new to me. This book presents the best of the columns I've written in my first two years with the *St. Paul Pioneer Press.*

I hope this collection will give you a smile, provide you companionship, raise awareness of issues and encourage you to become an advocate for women and physical activity. I believe that women who incorporate physical activity into their lives at any level will gain a broader perspective on life . . . and their own dreams and possibilities.

— *Judy Mable Lutter*

# Acknowledgements

Thanks to Judy Remington, who has become my mentor and friend since she's been editor of the *Melpomene Journal*. She has taught me how to say what I really want to say. Without Judy's encouragement and editing skills, this book would have been impossible.

I have been very lucky to have the talents and enthusiasm of numerous Melpomene volunteers and interns whose research and information gathering have contributed greatly to my columns. Thanks to Margie Boler, Julie Carlson, Krista Jordheim, Maren Patterson, Sarah Perry, Holly Pfitsch and Anne Snyder.

Thanks to my writing friends who provided encouragement and helped select the columns for the book: Barbara Andersen, Lael Berman, Florence Chambers and Martha Saul. Special thanks to Lael for her trademark wit and insight, which she used to come up with the title of the book and many of the essays. Thanks to Marilynn Taylor and Florence Chambers for their astute and careful proofreading.

I thank Susan Abbott of Abbott & Abbott and Sheila Oien of Write Design for their wonderful design ideas. The book's cover and section titles were designed by Susan and the interior pages are based on a design by Sheila. I thank Hilary N. Bullock for her beautiful photographs.

Thanks to Mike O'Malley, *St. Paul Pioneer Press* sports editor, and Jim Smith, deputy sports editor, for giving me the chance to write about women and sports and for their support of this book.

*This book is dedicated to my family: Hap, Wendy, Reid and Parke Lutter. They have encouraged me to follow my dreams. Their love, support and good humor have made all the difference.*

# HEROES

*Heroes*

# Sixty-Four and Still Going Strong

I SAT IN THE AUDIENCE RECENTLY TO APPLAUD A GOOD friend. The award she received, in recognition of years volunteering to ensure that more women would participate in physical activity, was long overdue.

Surrounded by other women and men gathered to celebrate women's accomplishments in athletic endeavors, I realized what Diane symbolizes. She is important not only because of her volunteer achievements but also as an example of what has changed for women in the past decade. Women have always volunteered, but we haven't always seen ourselves as athletes.

Diane began running at forty-eight. Like many of us who began to run later in life, she started out with old tennis shoes and few expectations. At first she didn't run very far, but a year later someone talked her into entering her first race. To her great surprise, she won her age division. Another important outcome for Diane was the chance to meet a whole new group of friends.

Few women ran in the late 1970s; even fewer tried competition. In 1975, only three women ran in the City of Lakes Marathon, the precursor to the Twin Cities Marathon. As the numbers grew, several women began to invite friends to run together. The creation of the Northern Lights Running Club provided a catalyst for women of all ages and abilities to join together for social runs, camaraderie and food.

Diane was typical of many Northern Lights members. She believed she could be a serious competitor and also play a significant organizational role as a race volunteer. Hers became a familiar face at the registration table, in the finish-line chute, handing out bananas. She became the race director for several women's events. No matter what her role, you were sure to be cheered by her smile and her heartfelt "You were great out there today!"

My first encounter with Diane was when she applauded my efforts. Once I knew the name attached to the smile, I also began to notice the name "Diane Goulett" appeared as an age-group winner in almost every race. But as she is quick to point out, "There weren't many of us 'old ladies' competing then!"

Competition offers Diane many rewards. One is the chance to see friends and make connections in a running community that doesn't focus on age or ability. It's a chance to make a significant volunteer contribution, something Diane has more time for now that she has retired from the Minneapolis public schools, where she was a speech pathologist. She's also serious about improving. She attends weekly speed workouts. She still strives to place in her age division, an increasingly difficult achievement as more older women enter competitions.

Diane inspires me. She's ten years older than I and going strong. She tells me that heading out the door to meet friends every morning for a four-mile run puts her day in perspective.

I hope I'm still running as far and fast as Diane when I'm sixty-four. More important, like Diane, I hope I'm still making a difference. Diane is not afraid to be visible. She stands out at the starting line and the finish line. It's hard to resist when she phones to ask you to help at a race. She convinces a lot of people that being physically active is a positive feature of growing older. Her example as a competitor and volunteer deserves applause and emulation.

# *Wheelchair Athlete Finds Joy and Challenge*

M Y MOTHER SPENT THE LAST NINE YEARS OF HER LIFE NOT far from her wheelchair. We were stunned when she suffered a massive stroke just before her sixty-fourth birthday.

Before that, swimming had been her great love, but she also had learned to play golf in her mid fifties. Not only did she love the game, she found she had natural talent. We envisioned her winning trophies on her eightieth birthday.

Life changes dramatically after a major stroke. My mom's most frustrating loss was the ability to speak completely and comprehensively. Another blow was the loss of her independence; she could no longer drive a car or hit a golf ball.

She could continue to swim. It wasn't with the grace of her earlier years, but swimming relaxed and refreshed her. Yet I knew her heart was sad when she saw the rest of the world being physically active.

My mother's disability taught me a lot about life for wheelchair users. In 1978, wheelchair accessibility was often a joke. Minnesota was just beginning to make cutouts on curbs; maneuvering in stores and museums was a challenge. Even worse was the treatment from strangers. Most scurried out of the way or ignored us. Others were patronizing or seemed to assume that anyone in a wheelchair was stupid and helpless.

Some of my younger friends who use wheelchairs say

they've encountered similar attitudes. That's why I have particular admiration for the young person with physical disabilities who lives a full life. Judy Siegle is such a person. In 1979, just after graduation from high school, Judy was riding in a car that was hit by a drunk driver. Judy's neck was broken; she became a quadriplegic. She was told she would never walk again. With perseverance and dedication, she has defied the odds.

Before her accident, athletics were a big part of Judy's life. She was on the all-conference girls basketball team for three years, and she was selected for the 1979 Minnesota all-state team. The lessons she learned from sports, including persistence and hard work, were key elements in her lengthy struggle to regain strength and independence.

After completing a master's degree, Judy decided to use her personal experience and professional training to help others who become disabled cope with the changes in their lives. She works in the social services department at MeritCare Hospital in Fargo, North Dakota, with patients who have suffered strokes, head injuries and spinal cord injuries.

Immediately following the accident, Judy's physical activity was related to her recovery. Now, she tries new sports for fun and because they increase her sense of strength and independence. She enjoys road racing, quad rugby, alpine sledding, tandem bicycling and downhill skiing.

Judy accentuates the positive. She admits there are many challenges when using a wheelchair, but she is determined not to be stopped by her disability.

The twelfth annual Kaiser Roll, to be held in Bloomington, Minnesota, in July, will highlight athletes like Judy who find joy and challenge in physical activity. Go cheer them on. Women like Judy Siegle teach us that physical disability does not define our capabilities. She encourages all of us to overcome barriers, no matter what our age.

# *Encouragement from Men Makes a Big Difference*

S OMETIMES IT'S THE MEN IN OUR LIVES WHO PROVIDE THE encouragement that women need to become physically active. That certainly was true for me.

I knew of no female role models when I started running. I simply headed out the door that first time to find some breathing space. I knew that my spouse, Hap, was always refreshed when he returned from his runs.

"Problems and frustrations seem less formidable on a run," he'd said. "I think they take on their proper perspective."

When Hap saw me enjoying the same benefits from running, he encouraged me to find time to run every day.

At first, we rarely ran together. We didn't plan it that way, but it probably was good that I started running by myself. Many women say they feel frustrated or inadequate if they start running or biking with a man.

I was lucky, however, to have a spouse who was not trying to prove anything by running with me. As I became a more seasoned runner, we started taking longer runs on Saturdays. We discovered it was a great chance to talk without interruption. We discussed problems that needed reflection. More important, it became a time to share ideas and dreams.

Before I started running, I'd been the accompanying spouse — encouraging Hap, impressed with his dedication and training. I shared his exhilaration at the finish of the race. But for many years I thought it was an unobtainable goal for me. Hap encouraged me to think otherwise.

Once I made the decision to try running a marathon, one of the biggest concerns was finding time to train. Our kids were young then. By juggling schedules, Hap and I both put in longer miles and decided to run the marathon together. When the day came, I approached the race with some trepidation.

The weather made it a challenging first marathon. The race started at noon and the temperature reached eighty-seven degrees before we crossed the finish line. Still, the first miles zoomed by, and Hap's experience at the distance kept us going at a steady pace. By mile twenty-three, however, I was fried. I knew I wasn't thinking clearly when I dumped two cups of Gatorade over my head, thinking it was water.

I came very close to quitting, but I didn't. The decision to continue was entirely mine, but Hap assured me that he was sure we could finish. The secret of my success that day was that I ran with someone I knew and trusted.

That belief in my ability, along with providing support so that I continue to take new risks and chances in all areas of my life, is characteristic of Hap. There are many spouses and dads who take great pleasure in applauding and cheering. Many realize women's opportunities have been limited in the past. They're the ones who wait at the finish line and provide support for women's events. We need to recognize the important role they play.

During hard races and on hard days, the encouragement and support I receive from Hap Lutter makes a huge difference.

# *Grandma Carlson Is Still Running "Grandma's"*

I F YOU'RE WATCHING THE MARATHON TODAY, DON'T GO inside after the front runners have passed. Some of the most impressive participants will be near the middle or end of the pack.

I always wait until I see my friend Mary Lou Carlson pass my house at mile twenty-two. Her arrival is announced by yells of encouragement from many bystanders. She's one of the best, and her fame is widespread in the running community.

Mary Lou has become a role model for hundreds of women since she began running fourteen years ago at the age of fifty-three. When her spouse, Howie, first started running, Mary Lou snuggled up with a book and thought he was a little crazy. When she first ran out the door, it was in old tennis shoes and pedal pushers.

Several weeks later, she saw a friend grocery shopping immediately after completing the Bonne Bell 10K race. Mary Lou was impressed. "I figured I'd be taking a nap after racing such a long distance," she said.

Only seven months later, friends convinced her to give racing a try. No one computerized that race. Instead, participants were given a popsicle stick to turn in so that times and places could be recorded. Mary Lou took hers home, unaware of its meaning or her place.

That was the last time Mary Lou was naive about her finishing time or place. She discovered she had natural talent and a competitive nature. Soon she was winning first place in her age division and setting state and national records. She joined a speed-training group. She started encouraging others.

Mary Lou ran Grandma's, her first marathon, in 1982 at Duluth, Minnesota. As a spectator the year before, she'd envisioned herself crossing the finish line. "I thought it would be fun to tell future grandchildren I once ran a marathon," she said.

Once Mary Lou had completed a marathon, she decided it should become a regular challenge. As a result, Mary Lou is one of about one hundred people who have run all twelve Twin Cities Marathons. In addition, she has run ten Grandma's Marathons and marathons in Boston, New York and other states, for a total of twenty-seven. Her personal best of 3:37:42 was set at the 1984 Twin Cities Marathon, where she qualified for the Boston Marathon.

She almost missed running Grandma's Marathon in 1987, the year she turned sixty. Her son David had chosen that date for his wedding. Because Mary Lou was convinced she could win first place in her age division, she suggested the wedding date be changed. Her supportive son agreed. Now his two children, ages two and three, stand at the finish line to cheer her.

Mary Lou deserves our admiration. She's an outstanding competitor, and her enthusiasm for life and running is legend. Her reputation is enhanced by her volunteer contributions. She's a member of the Twin Cities Marathon board and has been in charge of distributing flyers along the twenty-six-mile race course for the past twelve years. The massive task does not overwhelm her. "I just start early recruiting volunteers," she said.

Mary Lou can make even hard work sound like fun.

One of her fans said, "At sixty-seven, she's still out there covering the distance. She's my inspiration."

# Retirement Can Pave the Way to Adventure

W HEN YOU THINK OF RETIREMENT, DOES ROCK CLIMBING or bicycling across Wyoming spring to mind?

Outdoor adventures always have been the spice of life for Beverly Anderson. Bev retired from 3M Company at fifty-five to give herself time for as many adventures as possible. She's a role model for many women.

Bev has been pushing open doors and challenging the conventions of what women are supposed to do for many years. As a young woman in graduate school, she didn't see any other mothers pursuing an academic career. But she persevered anyway, earning a Ph.D. in cell biology while blazing a trail for the women who came behind her.

Bev doesn't think of herself as a trailblazer, nor does she regard herself as a natural athlete. "I was an awkward kid; I'm still an awkward adult," she said. "I don't have quick reaction time, but I've always liked to do things that make me tired. When the kids were little, I used to push them in the stroller for hours."

Bev was exposed to the running craze in her early thirties, while living in Oregon. She decided to give running a try and found she loved it. That's when she learned she was fast. When Bev moved to Minnesota, she was a formidable competitor. Whenever she raced for the 3M corporate team, she helped them win. It was a great frustration when a persistent sciatic nerve problem ended Bev's running career.

These days, you're most likely to find Bev biking or rock climbing. She insists rock climbing is easy to learn, even when you're in your sixties. Bev first wanted to rock climb at age six, but she couldn't convince her parents to let her try.

"Rock climbing is something that can be done at many levels of skill," she said. "It's important to learn technique, but that's easy to do in the Twin Cities. You don't have to be talented to do it safely and have fun." Bev often heads for Devil's Lake in Wisconsin for the best rock climbing in the Midwest.

When Bev isn't climbing, she's biking. To keep in shape for big adventures, including two "Ride around Wyoming" trips, she rides weekly with about forty women known as the Tuesday Group. She's formed friendships with many of the women who have been riding together for the past twenty years.

The informal structure is one key to the group's longevity. After each ride, one woman volunteers to set the route for the next Tuesday. A typical ride is thirty to sixty miles. Because the women live throughout the Twin Cities metro area, the routes are varied. Crucial to the planning is a good restaurant for a leisurely lunch to cap off the morning. The group flourishes because it provides incentive as well as camaraderie and fun.

Several of the group's members have been part of a twelve-year Melpomene study tracing the lifestyle patterns of women between the ages of fifty-seven and eighty-three. Based on a recently completed questionnaire on motivation, the social aspects of physical activity rank high on the list.

What keeps Bev active? The camaraderie of friends and the challenge of new rocks or a new bike route. She heartily advocates early retirement. It has given her time to enrich her marriage, enjoy her grandchildren and explore the joys of physical activity.

# No Mountain Is Too High for Billmeier

M EET SARAH BILLMEIER OF YARMOUTH, MAINE, A COM-
petitive national and international ski racer. Sarah was
named to the U.S. Disabled Ski Team at thirteen. In the 1992 and
1994 Paralympics, she won five gold medals and one silver. In the
last two seasons, Sarah has won a total of six gold medals at the
U.S. Disabled National Championships.

Sarah dominates the ski slopes of the world on one leg.
Her left leg was amputated above the knee due to cancer in her
hip when she was five years old. A series of operations removed
the cancer and left a stump. The stump has caused her more
trouble recently than her good leg. She has broken a bone in her
stump twice in the past eighteen months, once just two months
before the Paralympic games in Lillehammer, Norway.

Sarah began skiing at eight. Everyone in her family is a
recreational skier; her younger brother is a very good cross-
country skier. "From the beginning I just skied for fun," Sarah
said, "but subconsciously, I think I knew I would be wanting to
ski for a long time. I got a coach the very first day."

One of the reasons Sarah has been so successful is that
she continually strives to do better. "I was born with the love of
skiing, but technique must be learned," she said. "It requires both
physical and mental training." She also minimizes the difference
between able-bodied skiers (nicknamed "normies") and "gimps."

"Any good ski racer puts all of their weight on one ski in a turn, so it's essentially the same for me," she said. One difference between Sarah and a skier with two legs is her use of outriggers, which are ski poles with a short ski on one end that function like a ski pole plant. But Sarah can ski without either poles or outriggers.

Why? Because the key element in all levels of skiing, according to Sarah, is balance. It's something she works on every day. Another key element is speed. "You can't be scared of going fast, because then it's more dangerous," she said.

Sarah builds her confidence and skills by attending Green Mountain Valley School in Sugarbush, Vermont, a prep school that focuses on ski racing. Sarah benefits from the coaching she receives at the school as well as that provided by the Paralympic organization. Although the U.S. team is number one in the world, it is underfunded, and most skiers train on their own.

Sarah's training and dedication have made her a skier to admire. Lacy Danziger, writing in *Skiing* magazine, reminds us that talented disabled skiers are simply great athletes. "One of the amazing things about watching disabled skiers like Sarah is how inured your eye becomes to their disabilities," Danziger said. "The initial shock of seeing a strong, graceful, slender young woman whose leg is missing from the thigh down quickly recedes once you witness her confidence, poise and drive."

It was clear from interviewing Sarah that she puts life in proper perspective. Asked about her early bout with cancer, Sarah said she doesn't dwell on it. "I'm sure it helped shape my character, but I'm not preoccupied with the fact that it happened," she said.

Sarah is planning ahead but is not sure where competitive skiing will fit in her life over the long run. She'll enter Dartmouth in the fall with the goal of becoming a doctor. "That's been my dream ever since I can remember," she said.

# *Capitalizing on Capabilities*

S OMETIMES THE TEACHER BECOMES THE STUDENT. THE older I get, the more often that's true for me.

My first job was teaching high school. In subsequent years, I became a college instructor, a teacher of mentally challenged young adults and an intern supervisor. Teaching remains one of my loves. Because I have a sense of what it takes to be a good teacher, I'm impressed with excellence.

My friend Linda Bunker is such a teacher. I first knew her as a student, a sophomore in my honors history class. I soon became aware of not only her intelligence but also her wit and perseverance.

I knew Linda better than most of my students. She was a junior class officer, and I was the advisor. Linda was also a member of the Girl Scout troop I led. She was a nationally ranked junior tennis player, a fact that escaped my attention because there were no organized sports for girls in the high school.

We lost touch after her graduation. Twenty years later, our paths crossed again. We had lots of catching up to do. Linda had earned her Ph.D. in motor learning and sport psychology and was teaching at the University of Virginia.

In recent years, Linda has received national recognition for her outstanding contributions to girls and women in sport. She has authored thirteen books, published more than fifty research articles and presented more than two hundred papers at scientific and professional meetings.

Now associate dean for academic and student affairs at the University of Virginia, Linda is known for her ability to listen and mentor. Colleague Ann Boyce said, "Dean Bunker is one of the busiest people I know, but she never appears to be in a hurry and always has time for the next person who walks through her door. She has the uncanny ability to draw the very best out of those around her."

Linda is also known for her optimism and courage. These days, she needs both of those in abundance as she fights with cancer of the spine. Throughout her ordeal, she has remained an active teacher and advocate of the importance of sports. She credits her training in sport psychology and her competitive career with developing in her the skills necessary to survive her illness.

In the past, Linda excelled at golf and tennis. Now she teaches others from her wheelchair. Last year, after surgery that left her in full-time need of a wheelchair, she attended a tennis camp.

"The camp was wonderful," she said. "I was humbled by my clumsiness with the wheelchair but excited by the new skills I was learning."

Linda said the camp reinforced her belief that you must capitalize on your capabilities. "I try to forget what I can't do," she said. "I believe a strong athlete is an equally strong person. You do what you can with what you are given."

Linda has become my mentor as well as my friend. I admire her courage; I'm amazed at her optimism. She quotes a sport psychology maxim, "Attitude is the decision."

"It sounds almost trite," she says, "but it works for me. Ultimately, I decide what life will be like."

Linda has always decided to be a winner, no matter what the odds. Her life encourages others to be the best they can be.

# Balance and Focus Characterize Joan Benoit Samuelson

I HAVE FEW SPORTS HEROES. I ADMIRE THE ACHIEVEMENTS of several who excel at their sport, but many seem one-dimensional, or too young.

That's what makes Joan Benoit Samuelson so special. I vividly remember watching her running alone on the foggy Los Angeles freeway on her way to the first Olympic marathon medal ever awarded to a woman. She looked utterly determined and focused. I knew she had recently undergone arthroscopic surgery of her knee; her perseverance amazed me.

She became the hero of many people that day. Now you can learn more about her through a book published by Rodale Press. *Joan Samuelson's Running for Women,* co-authored with Gloria Averbuch of the New York Road Runners Club, combines research and personal tips for women runners of all ages.

The book is full of information on nutrition, menstrual cycle and pregnancy issues. It also provides tips on how to get started, train, race and avoid injuries. It's evident the two authors did their homework in working with experts in various disciplines. The most appealing aspect of the book, however, is its personal tone.

It is estimated that there are more than thirteen million women runners. While few, if any, will achieve Joan's accomplishments, there are many who can relate to the way she lives her life.

When Joan won the Olympic gold medal in the first-ever marathon for women in 1984, she was single and twenty-seven years old. Now a wife and mother of Abby, age eight, and Anders, five, she finds that running is only one part of a busy life. "Life is truly a balancing act," Joan writes in her book. "In one hand you hold your running, and in the other you hold your job, family and other daily tasks and challenges. For all the things that are important in your life, you have to find that balance."

Balance is the theme of Joan's book. She's a loving mom who writes, "Children keep you honest. They make you realize what your priorities really are or at least what they ought to be. Once the stopwatch was important for checking splits or a training pace; now I check my watch to pick up the children at school or meet a babysitter."

Joan also talks about the importance of having a focus beyond her family, of the need and desire to continue to challenge herself. She is still a competitor. She writes, "I set my sights on a sub-2:20 marathon — a goal that still sustains and motivates me. And whether I achieve that sub-2:20, I'd like to be part of the competition when it happens."

When Joan received the Melpomene Outstanding Achievement Award in 1991, she said, "When Abby begins to sort out the kind of woman she wants to be, I hope she'll have before her, in me, an example of a woman who set her own priorities and was at peace with them. I hope she'll see a woman who did what she did for the joy of it and who met unexpected challenges with equanimity."

That's the woman you'll meet in this book. She's a hero.

# Accepting Limitations and Appreciating Small Steps

I'M GLAD MY FRIEND, EDITH MUCKE, IS WALKING AGAIN. She was one of the first people to teach me about the joys of walking, so I knew how much a recent serious foot injury was cramping her style.

Edith was my boss when I worked at the University of Minnesota. She had returned to school to complete her bachelor's, then master's degrees after her children were grown. She then became the university's director of Continuing Education for Women. The program, founded in 1957, encouraged women older than the traditional college age to return to classes. At first the older students were called the "rusty ladies," although most of them were only in their thirties and forties.

As director, Edith was a good role model. What impressed me most was her attitude toward living. Edith always accentuated the positive, and she made sure she began the day right, with a brisk walk.

"Fresh air and the outdoors are high on my list of the Great Good," Edith says.

As a child, Edith loved to play outdoors. "There was no such thing as structured exercise: no acrobatics, swimming or ballet classes," she said. "Spring meant roller skates, summer meant swimming, winter was for skiing and tobogganing on the big hill. I loved it all."

Until her mid sixties, Edith thought nothing of walking three miles around Lake Harriet and then going for a swim. When her daughter, Jane, started running, Edith bought running shoes, too. She was sixty-three. Although she gave running a good try, she confided to Jane that "you miss a lot when you run."

She decided to stick to her walking. "Walking alone gives me time for meditation and reflection," Edith said.

As director of Continuing Education for Women, Edith knew many of her students. The atmosphere of her classes invited camaraderie and sharing. "One of the things I noticed," said Edith, "is that those women who were leading active lives, both mentally and physically, were far more content with their lives than those who were sedentary." Edith practiced her belief that strong minds and bodies complement each other.

In the year of her eightieth birthday, Edith's memoir, *Beginning in Triumph,* was published. At her book-signing party, she quipped, "People have a mistaken idea of what it means to be eighty. Just because I'm eighty doesn't mean I should be going about in a walker."

Less than a year later, she was struggling with a walker because she'd injured her foot. Edith became more philosophical, looking forward to the day when she could once again be independent. She practiced short walks in her apartment with the goal of walking to do her errands. Her optimistic outlook was tempered, but it never was lost.

Edith is making excellent progress. She hasn't made it around the lake yet, but I know she will. Like many of my older friends, Edith is teaching me that aging brings vulnerability. I can see that the physical activity that is so much a part of my life may need to be altered.

Yet Edith also reminds me that "you can learn to accept the limitations of mind and body. With aging, there's a new joy and appreciation of small steps."

# *In Control with Incontinence*

O NE OUT OF EVERY TWENTY-FIVE PERSONS IN THE UNITED States is incontinent. Barbara Aspaas is one of them. Barbara, a reading recovery teacher and avid golfer, underwent chemotherapy and radiation treatment for ovarian cancer when she was forty-one. Radiation and surgery caused scarring around her urethra, making it difficult for her to hold in urine.

That greatly complicated her ability to be physically active.

"I used to be on the lookout for the location of the nearest restroom," Barbara told me. "I had to constantly think about the situations I would be in. Even swinging a golf club was enough movement to empty my bladder. I used to not drink anything before or during a round of golf."

Barbara was frustrated because doctors kept telling her she would just have to deal with it. "But," she said, "I was forty-three years old and not ready to 'deal' with incontinence for the rest of my life — I was too young."

Incontinence is the involuntary loss of bladder or bowel control severe enough to have social and hygienic consequences. Incontinence can be caused by a urinary tract infection, vaginal infection or irritation, constipation, medication, pregnancy, surgery, hormonal changes, weak pelvic muscles or inadequate nutrition and water.

Incontinence often is not discussed; many people suffer

in silence. Yet, one out of six women forty-five and older say they suffer incontinence, and 27 percent of women over seventy-five say it's a problem.

Jennie Rodlund, coordinator of "I Will Manage," an information and support program of HealthEast Midway Hospital in St. Paul, Minnesota, said that incontinence is one of the last taboos to come out of the closet. Only one out of every twelve people with incontinence seeks help.

"Many of the participants in our classes talk about carrying extra sets of clothing with them when they go out or not being able to sit on cloth-covered chairs," Rodlund said. "They tell us they are afraid to join exercise classes."

The Bladder Health Council reports that exercise is one of the two most common activities that women eliminate from their lives because of incontinence. The other is shopping. It is difficult for people who do not suffer incontinence to understand the lifestyle change one has to go through to adjust to it.

But Rodlund and Aspaas stress that help is available. There are a growing number of solutions. A primary recommendation is to do Kegel exercises, which strengthen the pelvic-floor muscles. They can be done inconspicuously and are easy to learn. Two phone numbers for information on the exercises and help with incontinence are (800) 252-3337 and (800) 237-4666.

Sometimes simple lifestyle changes are all that is needed. Changes in diet and medication often help. Biofeedback also is becoming a popular alternative. Physical activity itself can help control incontinence.

Barbara Aspaas found that subtle changes in her diet, biofeedback and Kegel exercises were all that was required to control her incontinence.

"I've been doing Kegel exercises every day for two years," she said. "Now I can play golf, teach and not worry that I'm going to have a problem. You do not have to live with a bad situation. You can get help."

# Mind and Body Work Best in Concert

V ISITING RUTH STRICKER IS ALWAYS A TREAT. I MADE A trip recently to see her newly enlarged facility, The Marsh: A Center for Fitness and Balance, in Minnetonka, Minnesota. The thirty-three thousand square foot addition more than doubles the original building, which was opened in 1985.

The building is beautiful. One of my first impressions was the homey feeling. You are greeted by windows and couches, not fitness equipment and high-gloss changing rooms. The building sits on the edge of untouched wetlands, and its windows look out on a combination of prairie grasses and wildflowers.

The site was carefully chosen. Ruth talks about "engaging each person's spirit with the almost impressionist feeling of the quiet, natural marsh." Ruth has always believed in the connection between the physical and psychological. "I'm not interested in helping the 'fitter' get more fit. I want to provide a space that encourages people to revitalize their minds as well as their bodies," she said.

Her philosophy is worth paying attention to. She believes that "real fitness involves the mental, spiritual and emotional, as well as the physical aspects of an individual's life." Ruth has tested those beliefs, both personally and professionally.

Ruth has *lupus erythematosus.* Living with the disease has given new meaning to the idea that mind and body are one. It has made her aware of the special benefits exercise can provide. The Marsh has always reached out to those with special needs. Its pools are designed for easy wheelchair access, and blind students, adolescents struggling with chemical dependency and physically disabled adults are an integral part of those served. The Marsh also appeals to people like me. I've never been impressed with fitness. I don't really care about my heart rate, my body fat or the number of push-ups I can do. Until I saw the Marsh, I avoided clubs like the plague.

In the 1980s, most other clubs scoffed at the idea that fitness involved the mental, spiritual and emotional. They concentrated instead on the physical fitness aspects. They promised to make life better by making you fitter. A lot of people assumed that meant you would also be happier.

Yet the dropout rates, especially for women, showed it wasn't working. Exercise became another task on an already too long list of things to do.

Women are particularly appreciative of Ruth's philosophy of "adding soft edges to hard bodies." It's great to hear Ruth encourage you to "take the work out of workouts."

She says, "Exercise by itself can strengthen the body against physical ills. It can also reduce anxiety and depression, as well as promote relaxation. Combining exercise with meditation can increase those psychological benefits."

Ruth has recently given scientific underpinning to her practical proof that "mindful" exercise has measurable benefits. Results of a two-and-a-half-year collaboration with Herbert Benson, M.D., of the Mind/Body Institute at Harvard Medical School, and James Rippe, of the University of Massachusetts Medical School, confirm that "mindful exercise elicits immediate, positive emotions — enthusiasm, alertness and self-esteem."

I was a believer before the studies. It's been clear to me since I became physically active that mind and body work best in concert. If you have trouble believing that, the Marsh could help convince you.

# *Ann Bancroft: A Hero Inside and Out*

A NN BANCROFT IS ONE OF MY HEROES. SHE CAPTURED MY imagination long before I met her. I didn't want to trade places, but I admired her determination and abilities. I closely followed coverage of her first big adventure, the 1986 Steger International Polar Expedition. I was thrilled when the word came that they had reached the North Pole.

The first time I met Ann, she appeared shy and almost embarrassed to be the center of attention. She tends to minimize her accomplishments. Others are much more likely to realize that her feats are out of the ordinary.

Ann has received many awards. Perhaps the most impressive was bestowed upon her recently when she was inducted into the National Women's Hall of Fame in Seneca Falls, New York. She was the first Minnesotan to be honored and only the fifth athlete (Billie Jean King, Wilma Rudolph, Babe Didrikson Zaharias and Helen Stevenson had been inducted previously).

Ann was amazed by the award, the setting and the ceremony, which allowed each recipient to speak to the group for five to ten minutes.

"I'm still on a high three weeks later," Ann said. "The power and legacy of the women's stories motivated and inspired me. There was a tremendous sense of how other women had blazed trails for me, even though their achievements were in different arenas. I feel like I'm standing on their shoulders."

Ann spends much of her time these days talking to school children. She's unique because she not only lets them share her adventure, she encourages them to dream. She hates it when kids or adults say to her, "I couldn't do what you did."

"In the first place," Ann said, "going to the poles wasn't all that difficult. There were hard days, but I was doing what I have always loved to do.

"I encourage kids not to compare themselves with others. If they think I'm extraordinary, it limits their dreams. When I'm with them, I let them know I had to plan. I talk about my challenges and encourage them to set their own goals."

She says she has learned important lessons listening to kids and often tells the story of a fifth-grade girl who sent her a valentine to wish her luck on her first expedition. The girl wrote that she hoped she could be as brave as Ann when she moved to a new school in a new neighborhood.

"Courage is relative to the risk-taker," Ann said.

Ann believes her polar expeditions are not her biggest achievements. "Those are what clearly bring the most acclaim, but they were easier than other things," she said. For instance, it was hard for her to become a teacher. She had a learning disability and struggled through school.

Ann is also honest about another difficult journey. "Coming out as a lesbian was also a long and sometimes painful process, but it is something that is important and makes me proud," she said.

I was energized by talking with Ann. She has the rare ability, characteristic of good teachers, to spread enthusiasm and excitement. She gave me new courage and hope to do the things I want to do. The folks at Seneca Falls knew what they were doing when they selected her for the Women's Hall of Fame.

# Hopes

# *Physical Activity Can Save Moms' Days*

M Y THREE GROWN KIDS LIVE OUT OF TOWN, SO I ENVY moms who have kids around to help them celebrate Mother's Day. It seems appropriate that there should be one day when kids say thanks to their moms. Many of us spend a lot of our lives trying to do right by our kids.

I remember days, especially when my kids were young, when I badly needed relief. Trying to balance all the parts of my life was often a challenge. My best form of escape was a run around the block; I knew I would be a much better mom on my return.

A recent invitation to speak at the Washington County Job Training Center in Minnesota made one thing clear: Some moms have it a lot tougher than I did. The women in my audience were all single mothers. Most were in their twenties, and all had at least one child. All were enrolled in a post-secondary education and training program so they could get good jobs. They want a better life.

I was invited to talk about taking time for yourself. I suggested that the best way was to find a half-hour a day to go for a walk or ride a bike. Yet I knew those moms faced incredible barriers. I listened carefully to their questions.

They asked how they could possibly take time for themselves. They questioned whether being physically active would really make a difference in the way they felt about themselves. They wondered what they could do with their kids while they exercised.

I told them what had happened to me about six months after I began running. I was fixing dinner; my four-year-old son, Parke, was hanging on my legs. "Mom," he said in a very grown-up voice, "have you run today?"

"No," I growled.

"I wish you would," came his reply. "You're really grouchy, and you're so much nicer after a run."

The women understood when I told them I figured I should pay attention if a four-year-old could see that exercise could relieve stress.

One young woman described her day: up at 6:30 A.M. and to bed at 11:00 P.M., with every moment in between programmed for school or child care.

"When I finally go to bed," she sighed, "I'm so tired I can't sleep. Dancing relaxes me, but how can I do that with my schedule?"

Someone suggested she put on a record and dance by herself. One woman said, "I've learned I just have to double up. That means I put the two kids in the wagon and take my notes along for a twenty-minute walk. It's not perfect, but it sure helps."

The women were eager to learn, eager to make changes. They also were realistic: Finding time for yourself isn't always practical. The best Mother's Day present for them might be an hour alone. It might be a bike ride. It might be someone calling to say, "Hang in there."

Most of the kids are too young to appreciate what their moms are trying to do. It may be a long time before they realize their moms are courageous, strong, tenacious, resilient and determined, but I'm betting that some day these kids will say thanks to their moms. While the odds are staggering, these women have dreams for themselves and their kids. Taking time to play gives them a better chance to succeed.

# *Girls Need to Know They Can Be Heroes*

M YRA AND DAVID SADKER'S BOOK, *FAILING AT FAIRNESS,* gives us a good clue about why girls find it difficult to imagine themselves as heroes able to make a difference.

High-school and grade-school students nationwide were given five minutes to name twenty famous American women from the past or present. The rules: no sports figures, no entertainers and only presidents' wives who were famous in their own right. When the question was posed, the kids thought it would be easy to answer. But when the question was asked of hundreds of students, no one came up with twenty names.

Why, ask the Sadkers, do boys and girls have so much trouble naming famous women? The most compelling reason is that students don't learn about women in the classroom.

I don't think the numbers would be much greater if you allowed students to include female sports heroes. Try it. Can you name twenty famous women athletes? Can you name five women who are sports heroes?

How about Marion Jones and Charlotte Smith? They play for the same North Carolina school as Michael Jordan did. Smith, an amazing athlete, made a three-point shot in the final seven-tenths of a second in the 1994 women's basketball Final Four, to give her team the title. She wears the same number as Jordan. You might think she chose that number because of his example. He has had a career worth emulating.

But that guess is wrong. Charlotte Smith chose number twenty-three because that was her mother's number. She's lucky to have a mom who was an athlete. Yet neither Charlotte's nor her mother's name and athletic achievements are likely to be remembered for very long.

We're more likely to remember male athletes' names because we expect to hear about them for years to come. We anticipate college is just the start of their sports career, rather than the end, as it most often is for female athletes.

Women's chances for fame and some fortune are limited to fewer arenas. Tennis, golf, occasionally the Olympics. Yet the fact that our stories are subsequently lost has major consequences: It makes for fewer possibilities and role models for girls and women.

Recent Melpomene Institute research shows that girls who participate in physical activity and sports are more self-confident. Additionally, playing sports helps them feel competent. But many girls tell us they lack role models.

Producer Jane Helmke and KARE-TV shared Melpomene's concern about the inability of girls to find role models or be a hero. In the video, "Heroes, Growing up Female and Strong," we explore some of the characteristics exemplified by athletes like Charlotte Smith. We identify women who dare to stand out, to excel. We speak of the need to be yourself, to be strong enough to prize who you are. We encourage girls to take chances and be a hero to others.

All of us need to identify outstanding women. We need to speak out in the media, in our schools and at home. If we don't, girls and boys won't change their idea of who belongs in the history books or sports pages.

Each of us can encourage girls we know to aspire to be the best they can be. Identifying heroes is a good way to start.

# Girl Scout Camp Emphasizes Physical Competency

M
Y EARLY SUMMERS WERE SHAPED BY THE TIME I SPENT AT camp. As soon as the Girl Scout summer camp catalogue arrived, I was ready to go.

As a second and third grader, I attended day camp and loved it. Spending all day outside — hiking, cooking over an open fire and playing games — was heaven. But I was also marking time, waiting until I was old enough to sign up for two full weeks of overnight camp.

By the end of fourth grade, I finally was able to go off to overnight camp, which proved to be all I had dreamed of. There were new kids to meet. There were counselors young enough to seem like older, admired sisters. Camp also taught me new skills and brought new adventures.

Swimming lessons were the highlight of the day for me. Even though my mom was an excellent swimmer, it seemed much easier to learn to swim with a "real" instructor. Moreover, as soon as you were an intermediate swimmer, you graduated from rowboats to canoes. For me, that was a big incentive to improve.

As I grew older, I begged to go to camp for four weeks. I looked forward to five-day canoe trips on the St. Croix River. In accord with the Girl Scout belief that girls should take the initiative, our leaders let us plan menus for our trips. Sometimes we goofed and found ourselves with ingredients on the trail that were pretty horrible. Our leaders made sure we didn't go hungry, but they knew mistakes often taught valuable lessons.

The camping scene has changed in the past thirty years. When I was a kid, our choices were limited to Girl Scout, YWCA or private camps. Today, there are many more camps, and they tend to be specialized. In addition to sports camps for basketball and baseball, there are computer and weight-loss camps. Many are now co-educational.

I think Girl Scout camp is still an excellent option. Many girls say they like being in a situation where they don't have to compare themselves with boys. One of the most positive features is the chance for girls to learn how competent they can be.

Physical competence is something that gets short shrift in our schools today. I recently talked with a group of fifth-grade Girl Scouts who reported having gym class one day per week. When this is the case, how can we expect kids of either gender to grow up thinking physical activity is important?

Sending them to a camp that emphasizes competency in the outdoors can help fill the gap. Camp Northwoods, owned and operated by the Girl Scout Council of St. Croix Valley, is such a camp. Taking advantage of the natural surroundings, the camp concentrates its programs on canoeing, backpack trips and water sports.

Three years ago, my daughter was a member of the camp staff. She assured me that the philosophy of helping girls make decisions was still strong. "It's fun to see girls change in just two weeks," she said. "Some who arrive feeling very hesitant about their abilities discover they are physically competent. There's something about a camp setting that allows girls to be open, to learn more about who they are."

I remember nights under the stars. The smell of a campfire will always bring memories of s'mores and songs. Most important, that's where I learned I could be a leader as well as a follower. I would go again in a minute.

# Strong Minds and Strong Bodies Complement Each Other

I APPLAUD THE "POWERFUL MESSAGES" CONFERENCE HELD recently at the Humphrey Institute in Minneapolis. The purpose was to recognize the importance of academics, to tell kids that doing well at their studies should be recognized and honored. The goal of the conference was to underline the connection between academic achievement and success.

Sometimes it appears we honor the athlete and ignore the student. It's just as dangerous to assume that someone who is brilliant and studious is automatically nonathletic. When I was in school, there were few choices. I was studious; I was not the cheerleader type. I do not remember high school fondly. I felt like an outsider and learned little about teamwork or leadership.

When I compare my experience with that of my kids, I think they came out ahead. Our daughter and two sons were high-school and college athletes. They were also good students. These two aspects of their lives complemented each other. They frequently got their best grades in the middle of their sports seasons.

It's the star athlete we usually read about. In some cases, particularly at the Division I collegiate level, some of the athletically talented struggle with their studies. Some may not be academically talented; many others have received the false message that their athletic skills will get them anywhere.

Recent rule changes are attempting to change that. It's becoming harder to be the athlete who just gets by, who never really gets enough credits to graduate from a university.

That's good, because I have a real problem with "using" kids. That's what the old system often did. It put young men on the basketball court for the pleasure of fans who cared most about a winning team.

Contrast this with the "student athlete," a concept and term that gives equal emphasis to academics and athletics. Student athletes are especially common in Division III schools — small colleges that are prohibited from offering athletic scholarships. In this kind of situation, there is much less likelihood of academics getting shortchanged.

When Melpomene Institute asked a group of female high school athletes whether competitive sports was a major factor in their choice of a college, most said no. Most female athletes do not expect college athletic scholarships, but many do want the opportunity to compete or to have facilities that would allow them to continue to stay in shape.

Many said they were trying to choose a college or university because it was a good fit — meaning academics, specific majors and affordablity. My daughter also made it a point on her college visits to talk with members of the track team and athletic department. She knew she was a better student when she was involved in sports.

Does it make a difference? I think it does. When faced with tough challenges in graduate school, our daughter credits some of her resilience and strength to her sports background. She has learned to work at solutions; she knows discipline contributes to success.

The bright kid who thinks all athletes are dumb loses out on life just as surely as the athlete who thinks he or she doesn't need to be a good student. Both are wrong. The best advice is to combine the two. Strong minds and strong bodies complement each other.

# All Work and No Play Is Hazardous to Our Health

P HYSICAL ACTIVITY AND SPORTS FOR WOMEN BOOMED IN the 1980s. Women bought running shoes, tennis racquets and bikes in unprecedented numbers. Sportswear manufacturers were delirious. They predicted a never-ending upward spiral.

It appears they were overly optimistic. New research indicates there has been a drastic reduction in physical activity. It is most pronounced among women under thirty-five.

Using statistical data from the National Center for Health Statistics based on interviews with 33,232 women in 1985 and 41,104 in 1990, Geoffrey Godbey, professor of leisure studies at Penn State University, and John Robinson, professor of sociology at the University of Maryland, document that physical activity for women under thirty-five has declined 16 percent. Physical activity for men of the same age has declined 9 percent.

Collecting data on physical activity is a challenge. Frequently, researchers base their conclusions on skimpy evidence. In this case, however, participants were asked what physical activities they had engaged in during the previous two weeks and how often they had engaged in each activity during that period. This kind of careful documentation produces numbers worth discussing.

Why are fewer people, especially younger women, exercising less?

Talking to my three twentysomething kids and their friends provides some explanations for the decline in physical activity. A big reason is employment. No matter what their educational level, it's tougher for this generation to find jobs.

The lean and mean stance of business in the '90s means that fewer people are working, and they're working longer hours. Once you land a job, there is pressure to prove you can work longer and harder than the next person. In *The Overworked American,* Juliet Schor documents that Americans have only sixteen and one-half hours of leisure per week. Our longer hours mean we work the equivalent of two months more than workers in West Germany. That's not healthy.

In a 1990 Melpomene membership study, 56 percent of women aged twenty to twenty-nine reported stress related to their jobs. Ninety-five percent said they knew physical activity reduced their overall stress level. But faced with deadlines, family responsibilities and daily chores, many said physical activity fell to the bottom of their priority list.

My twenty-seven-year-old daughter tells me she is often the exception. She continues to be physically active in spite of time constraints. As a result, she often finds herself the only woman in a group of men who are much more likely to make exercise a priority. She bemoans the fact that none of her female friends choose to spend their free time on a mountain bike or a pair of skis. Only one woman in her office occasionally joins her for a walk at noon.

Employers ought to take notice. Stress reduces productivity. Encouraging employees to take time during the workday for physical activity should become a priority. Otherwise, the problem will get worse.

Workaholic behavior is not healthy. The decline in physical activity for women impacts more than sporting manufacturers. As more women enter the workplace, we need to encourage them to strike a balance between work and play. If we don't, we'll need more than health-care reform to cure our problems.

# Basketball Clinic Helps Girls Shoot for Better Life

"IT'S A CHANCE FOR ME TO GIVE BACK TO MY COMMU-nity." "It's a sense of obligation; I want to share my great basketball experiences with younger girls." These statements are from Lisa Lissimore and Linda Roberts, two of the founders of the Shooting Stars basketball clinics, who saw a need that demanded their attention.

When Lisa was growing up in the 1970s, the Oxford playground in St. Paul offered a full program of sports for girls. Lisa credits those programs with giving her a solid background in sports. Returning to the playground in the summer of 1982, she was appalled that fewer programs were offered. She saw almost no girls shooting baskets.

Lisa, a star basketball player at St. Paul Central, now associate director of the State High School League, is a woman of action. She met with five friends, all African-American athletes who had profited from their experiences in the St. Paul and Minneapolis public schools, to find a solution. Girls in the Sum-mit-University neighborhood of St. Paul told them they weren't playing because they had to work. The available programs didn't fit their schedules; other basketball camps were expensive.

In response, these six women established a clinic that could reach out to girls in the neighborhood. They chose early evening hours and targeted girls aged eight to eighteen. Their goal was to emphasize more than competitive interaction, playing strategies and basketball rules. They believed fostering positive self-esteem in a supportive environment was crucial.

A typical evening includes an hour of goal setting, conditioning exercises and practicing various skills. Guest speakers are invited to give twenty-minute presentations focusing on either basketball, future goals and opportunities or self-esteem issues. The evening continues with more than an hour of one-on-one sessions, five-on-five competitions and individual and team contests. Finally, the girls discuss what motivates them to achieve team or individual goals.

These are characteristics of any good basketball camp. The uniqueness of the Shooting Stars clinic is its cost, location, targeted population and emphasis on positive role models. Costs are extremely low because all of the coaches volunteer their time. The Martin Luther King Center donates the space. The fees of $15 for girls eight to eleven and $20 for girls twelve to eighteen ensure wide participation. No one is turned away. "We somehow find a sponsor for anyone who wants to attend," said Lissimore.

A can-do attitude is characteristic. It's an important factor in the success of a program with a tiny budget. But the major ingredient is a sense of community.

"I had a good career in basketball," said Roberts. "I think more young girls should be given that chance. It helps build self-confidence and gives a girl a better chance for success in whatever she chooses to do."

There are many success stories. Several former clinic participants are Dave Winfield finalists or scholars; some have access to higher education because of basketball scholarships. Most important, each girl leaves the clinic knowing more about herself and her capabilities.

# *Long Vacations Are Rejuvenating*

THIS WEEK I'M ON VACATION. THAT'S SOMETHING AMERI-cans don't do often enough or long enough. For one thing, many of our employers don't encourage time off. European top management, in contrast, believes that rest and rejuvenation are essential not only for personal health but for the well-being of the company. I agree with the Europeans.

Yet I must remind myself often of the importance of rest. Several weeks ago as I was leaving the office for a long weekend trip to visit my son, Melpomene Institute's office manager asked if I was taking work along.

"Of course," I said, "the airplane is a great place to work without interruption."

"But," she persisted, "will you work once you're there?"

I thought I might, but it turned out that I didn't. As soon as I settled into the different rhythm afforded by being away, I found reading a book and trying new adventures filled the entire day. We went on a long mountain hike, ran, fly-fished, and ice skated on the famous Sun Valley outdoor rink.

It reminded me of the first real vacation I took, shortly after graduating from college. Two friends and I spent a long weekend at a resort in northern Minnesota. This was long before I considered myself an athlete. Neither of my friends was particularly athletic either, but the resort offered golfing, tennis, boating and, of course, a lake. We tried everything. Later we laughed at our frenetic pace. I was exhausted when I returned home.

My vacations changed when we began to go to Tunisia, North Africa, on a regular basis. When my husband volunteered as an orthopedic surgeon there, our first stay was for six months. For the next ten years after that, we returned for six-week periods.

Initially, my husband worked his usual ten-hour day. I was forced to adjust to a slower pace because I stayed home with our three kids. Our living quarters were always tiny. The kids' toys consisted of Matchbox cars, Legos, puppets and crayons — things that were small and easy to transport. We had lazy days of building sand castles and sitting on the beach. At first, the change of pace was stressful. It seemed unnatural to have unstructured time. I brought research with me and carved out a part of each day to work.

But we were intrigued with the Tunisian custom of *séance unique,* their term for a summer schedule. *Séance unique* meant working from seven o'clock in the morning until one in the afternoon and having the rest of the day free.

This schedule made sense. Tunisian summers are hot, with temperatures frequently in the high nineties. Air conditioning is rare. Tunisians know they aren't very effective in the heat and simply do the smart thing. They return home for an afternoon nap and a trip to the beach.

We ought to try that pattern in Minnesota. Putting a pause in each day beats roaring out for long weekends. But it doesn't diminish the need for long vacations. Long vacations remind us we don't need to be frenetically active.

As I settle into the slower vacation rhythm, I find myself not only refreshed but also more creative. I'm always surprised at the incredible energy generated by a long period away from my usual surroundings. When I return, I bring new perspectives and insight to my work.

# Eating Disorders Are Problems for All of Society

T HE DEATH OF CHRISTY HENRICH PRODUCED MANY headlines. Christy, a world class gymnast, died in July 1994, of complications from anorexia nervosa and bulimia.

Media attention was immediate. "Among Female Athletes, Eating Disorders Are On Rise" was the headline in the August 1, 1994, *New York Times.* "Dying to Win: For Many Women Athletes the Toughest Foe Is Anorexia" headlined a special report in the August 8 issue of *Sports Illustrated.*

These headlines disturb me. Once again, women athletes received lots of media attention for the negative side of sports. I'm concerned parents will decide athletics are dangerous for their daughters. This is far from true.

But the issue is complex. We need coverage of the problems of anorexia and bulimia. Eating disorders can lead to death. It is important for coaches and parents to be aware that young athletes may be particularly sensitive about weight. Christy's mom said that it was a gymnastics judge who first told Christy that she was too fat. Christy's response was to start dieting in earnest.

Six years ago, the issue of eating disorders was not routinely discussed by coaches. Many coaches weighed their athletes regularly, and there was a subtle if not overt message that thin was better.

Some athletes get hooked on losing weight because they

believe it will improve performance. In some sports, performance is related to appearance. Gymnastics, diving and figure skating are prime examples. Further, the media deliver the message that thin is better. The press has a history of making disparaging remarks about Tanya Harding's "thunder thighs." Every article I read about Jennifer Capriati several years ago suggested she was getting chubby. Yet I saw no evidence that either young woman's performance was hindered. I saw two superb athletes who were being criticized because they weren't skinny.

Let's look at the real issue. Anorexia and bulimia are on the rise in the general population. The desire to be ultrathin is not limited to athletes. That's a critical message. In a February 1994 column, Ellen Goodman reports that "at any moment more than half of adolescent girls and three-fourths of adult women describe themselves as on a diet." A 1994 *Esquire* Poll found that 50 percent of women aged eighteen to twenty-five would rather be dead than fat. Ninety-eight percent of girls in a Minnesota high school recently reported that weight issues and the desire to be thin were concerns for them.

The Association of Anorexia and Associated Disorders estimates that 18 percent of females suffer from anorexia and bulimia. Most eating disorders start during the teen years. Six percent result in death.

We need to be concerned because it's a societal problem, not an athletic one. Until we stop thinking that women who look like starved refugees are beautiful, until girls and women start to believe they are worthy no matter what their body shape and size, we are in big trouble.

As long as self-esteem for women is closely tied to weight, we will have an increase in the number of women who develop eating disorders. Awareness and education can be keys to change. Because of a new understanding of the problem in the athletic community, girls with eating problems have a better chance to get help early on.

# Physical Activity Helps Women with Breast Cancer

I
F YOU ARE FORTY-FOUR, IN GREAT PHYSICAL SHAPE AND eat a healthy diet, you don't expect to be diagnosed with breast cancer. When Linda Brown Harris decided she should have her baseline mammogram, she was not worried. Yet she was among the roughly 1 percent of women diagnosed with breast cancer by the age of forty-five. The one-in-nine statistics so often quoted are true for women by the age of eighty-five.

While breast cancer is not the leading cause of death for women, it is a disease that evokes great fear, especially among younger women. When Linda received her diagnosis, she lowered her anxiety level by searching for the best information. She explored the positives and negatives of lumpectomy and mastectomy. During this tense period, she continued to play tennis and golf as a way to relieve her stress.

Linda was fortunate. Her cancer was detected at an early stage. She found a lot of information in her search for the best course of treatment for her to follow, but she was also frustrated. She realized she needed a guide to help her focus and think clearly. She felt the need to raise crucial questions when talking with her doctors and nurses.

Linda is a woman of action. During her recovery period, she began to write the book she wished had been available for her. The result is *Breast Cancer: A Handbook* (published by

43

Melpomene Institute), which helps women diagnosed with breast cancer know what key questions to ask their health-care providers. The book serves as a companion as a woman gathers information, understands her options and makes decisions about her treatment and self-care. Further, it is a guide for her family and friends, who also face stress when breast cancer is diagnosed.

Linda knew that her belief in the importance of physical activity shaped some of her decision making and helped her physical and emotional recovery. But there is very little research on physical activity and its relationship to breast cancer.

To begin to fill the void, a questionnaire was included at the back of *Breast Cancer: A Handbook*. Women are asked to complete the questionnaire four months or more after treatment has begun. While the sample size is still small, the results suggest the importance of physical activity.

Seventy-five percent of the responses Melpomene has received report that physical activity was very important or extremely important to their overall sense of well-being. One woman said physical activity was important because "I feel better. In the time between diagnosis and surgery, the only times I felt good were when working out."

Half of the women had experienced no obstacles to being physically active since their treatment; for the others, pain and discomfort were the biggest obstacle. Most of the women returned to their previous levels of physical activity in spite of obstacles because it was important to their recovery. They said it was especially important in regaining a feeling of control.

Women faced with breast cancer need to know more about their options. They do not find their health-care professionals very knowledgeable when it comes to answers about physical activity. By sharing experiences, women not only help themselves but also expand the knowledge base for others.

# Comfortable Clothes Encourage Physical Activity

I T HAPPENS RARELY NOW. IT SURPRISES ME WHEN IT DOES. Last week I was running along, enjoying the scenery, when two young men whistled from their car. I was old enough to be their mother and chose to ignore them.

But when I'm running with younger friends, I get angry when boys and men think it's okay to comment and whistle when girls and women run by. Maybe that's why I like the Coke ad in which women ogle a man. It's aroused a lot of comment, both positive and negative. Some women take the high ground: If we don't like it, we shouldn't do it to men. As far as I can tell, we've been saying we don't like it for years. That hasn't stopped most of them.

Fifty years ago, almost everyone thought it was inappropriate for women to engage publicly in physical activity. My grandmother told me it was inappropriate for a lady to wear shorts once she reached the age of ten. Looking proper was important to her. She always wore a dress and hoisery. She sewed me frilly dresses that I grew to hate.

I didn't agree with her clothing rules, but I admired my proper grandmother. Her desire to attend college on a music scholarship had been denied by her parents. She was glad I'd have broader opportunities. She respected my intelligence and taught me to think for myself.

Not surprisingly, sports were not part of her upbringing. She didn't actively discourage me from camping and biking, but I know she was just as glad she didn't have to see me in action.

What would she think if she were to see me running through the streets in my shorts at the ancient age of fifty-four? She'd probably be shocked and embarrassed. But times have changed. More women beyond the age of fifty are trying adventures that would have been frowned upon not many years ago.

Some women are still hesitant to try a sport or physical activity because they think they will attract negative attention. Twenty years ago, a friend in her fifties discovered the joy of running. For several years she stayed indoors, running in the early morning hours on the dirt track at the University of Minnesota. She routinely sweltered in men's sweatpants. When she complained about the heat and an allergic reaction, I invited her to join me outdoors.

"Never!" was her emphatic reply. "There is no way I would expose this body in public."

Many women don't want to invite comment or whistles, but they do want to have clothes that look good and feel comfortable. Ellen Wessel, president of Moving Comfort clothes, decided to start her own company in 1977 because, she said, she was "tired of running in men's clothing that chafed, rode up, fell down and generally exposed more than my running ability."

At first, it was tough to compete with well-established companies, but once women discovered the superior fit, comfort and performance of Moving Comfort clothes, they helped spread the word.

If my grandmother had heard about these clothes, she would have had to reconsider her rules. I bet she would have done more than her occasional walk around the block if she hadn't always been wearing her skirt and heels.

These days, we are just as entitled as men to go out to run, walk or ride our bikes without being hassled. Comfortable, attractive clothes encourage us to be physically active.

# *Work of Women Sportswriters Makes for Spirited Reading*

A RE YOU LOOKING FOR A GOOD BOOK? ONE OF THE BEST I've read recently is *A Kind of Grace*, a collection of ticles written by women sportswriters.

I bought the book shortly after it was published by Zenobia Press. It's the kind of book that fits a busy schedule. Because the book is a compilation of seventy-seven pieces by sixty-six women writers, it's easy to read a couple of articles at a sitting. But be forewarned: You'll find it hard to decide what to read first. The book includes a great variety and range of topics.

One of the strengths of the book is editor Ron Rapoport's appreciation of the sexism inherent in the culture of sports and the world of sportswriting. He estimates there are more than two hundred women sportswriters. Those numbers have not been easily achieved. When Susan Reimer and two other women arrived at the Baltimore Orioles clubhouse in 1979, the manager of the team said they couldn't come in without notes from their fathers.

In 1994, the Orioles asked Reimer to appear on an instructional video about media relations to explain to players the role of women sportswriters. "In my videotape," Reimer told a *Baltimore Sun* reporter, "I explained that women become sportswriters for pretty much the same reason men do. They like sports, and they like to write. I explained that women sportswriters want to be in the locker rooms and clubhouses because that's where the athletes are."

Because the priorities of most sports page readers are baseball, football and basketball, many ambitious and talented women choose to focus on these sports. Some, however, have found a niche reporting about women. The *Minneapolis Star Tribune* recently suggested that a woman writing about women and sports was a form of segregation. I disagree.

So does Rapoport, who believes that the stories women bring to the sports pages often reflect experiences and perceptions men cannot share. Yet the telling of those stories helps men and women gain a clearer appreciation of the benefits of women's and girls' participation in sports.

I would have been disappointed if the book had not included Jacqui Banaszynski's description of her love affair with basketball, which appeared in the *St. Paul Pioneer Press* on March 19, 1987. I remember reading it the day it was published. I cried then, and it still brings tears to my eyes when I reread Jacqui's article about girls competing in the state high-school tournament.

"You see, I could have been a player too," she writes. "I was born with all the right features . . . height, heft, heritage and heart. . . . My mother was a farm girl who believed it was okay to sweat. My four brothers were brutal under the boards. They taught me to fake with my eyes and to make space with my elbows.

"Basketball was a family tradition, a neighborhood social event, a reprieve from homework, a physical outlet for the emotional intensity of adolescence. But that's all basketball ever was for me, and my game never left the driveway. Because I was born female, and I was born too soon."

*A Kind of Grace* makes you contemplative, sad, exhilarated and, finally, happy to be female in a sports world that has grown more friendly over the past decade. Sections on milestones and pioneers, sexual harassment, racism, homophobia and coaching only begin to describe the book's diversity. But don't take my word for it — get it for yourself.

# In-Shape Women Come in All Sizes

N EW STATISTICS INDICATE THAT WE ARE GROWING EVER fatter. The Centers for Disease Control and Prevention reports that between 1971 and 1991 the proportion of American adults characterized as obese or 20 percent over their ideal body weight increased from one-quarter to one-third.

Is this necessarily bad news?

What if we changed our focus? Instead of worrying about numbers on a scale, what if we could convince people, women in particular, that you could be healthy and fat, at the same time? It's not a preposterous idea. Dr. Reuben Andres of the National Institute of Aging says the "major studies of obesity and mortality fail to show that obesity leads to greater risk."

But the general medical and popular belief is that fat is not only unhealthy but also unattractive. Being fat has serious social consequences. A University of Florida survey of people who had once been overweight said they would rather lose their sight, their hearing or a leg than be overweight again. Yet most diets fail.

What if large women stopped trying to lose weight or diet and decided instead to become physically active? Unfortunately, it's not that easy. Fat women face many prejudices. Some are translated directly into obstacles that make participation in physical activity very difficult.

Melpomene Institute became interested in the issues of larger women and physical activity in 1988. Talking with larger women convinced us that we should encourage physical activity without linking it to weight loss. Melpomene research discovered that many women had not begun an exercise program because they were afraid of ridicule. One woman who formerly played tennis said she stopped because she became "embarrassed by [her] size."

Think about it. How often have you said, "She's too big to be wearing that swimsuit," or, "A woman her size can't possibly be a runner." You should meet Lynn Cox, who holds many world long-distance swimming records and says weighing 209 pounds is a key to success in her sport.

You should talk to Pat Lyons, a nurse educator in San Francisco who promotes physical activity for large women. She speaks from personal experience. She's the rare woman who talks openly about carrying 240 pounds on her 5'8" frame.

As a kid, Pat loved physical activity. When diet after diet failed, she decided to become physically active again for the pleasure it provided, not for the weight loss possibilities. She looks and feels much better now that she exercises daily. She also persuaded her employer, Kaiser Permanente, to sponsor classes emphasizing the health benefits of physical activity regardless of size.

I no longer make assumptions about weight and health. I know a few skinny women who starve themselves to maintain what they think is an ideal body. I suspect the fat woman who walks daily or swims four times a week is healthier. I speak out when friends make comments about women fatter than themselves. We're all born different. Large women have just as much right as anyone else to be exercising.

# Exercise Makes Each Day Better

A N APRIL 1994 *NEW YORK TIMES* ARTICLE CAUGHT MY EYE. It reported that the most common outdoor activity for Americans was "driving for pleasure."

The data was gathered in a Roper Starch poll that had a very low margin of error. Respondents were asked to tell the interviewers if they had participated in various activities at least once in the past year. After "driving for pleasure," reported by 40 percent, the outdoor activities cited were swimming (35 percent), picnicking (33 percent) and fishing (26 percent).

Does that sound like a fit society? In May 1995, Jim Warren concluded in the *St. Paul Pioneer Press* that the fitness movement had never happened. It's time to reexamine the reasons for physical activity. Is there a truly effective way to encourage exercise?

The collective moaning about Americans' lack of fitness usually is tied to our increasing girth. Women in particular are concerned about weight. Numerous researchers consistently find that losing or maintaining weight is a major reason women consider an exercise program. Unfortunately, the hype that suggests physical activity will result in significant weight loss is false.

One of the problems with the fitness movement or the admonitions to get off the couch is that expectations are often unrealistic. Further, the news about how much exercise is necessary has changed at least twice in the past year. A study reported in the April 19, 1995, issue of the *Journal of the American Medical Association* found that only vigorous exercise reduced the risk of dying. Only men were studied.

At first glance, this seems to contradict the guidelines issued earlier this year by the Centers for Disease Control and the American College of Sports Medicine, which recommended that thirty minutes a day of moderate activity, done all at once or in smaller increments, can produce significant health benefits.

The difference in the research and recommendations might be that one predicts living healthier; the other, living longer. The two are not necessarily identical.

I've always balked at the suggestion that target heart rates are a good way to prescribe or monitor exercise. To me, it equates physical activity with something that must be done. I agree with an article by R.K. Dishman in the *Journal of Medical Science and Sports Exercise,* which suggests that encouraging healthy adults to be physically fit throughout their lives might be achieved best by permitting them to select a "preferred intensity" for exercise.

Dishman writes, "Studies have shown that prescribing exercise intensity based on heart rate can be unsuccessful when the prescribed heart rate is not appropriate for physiologic reasons. In addition, when patients prefer a level of exercise that does not match what's been prescribed to them, they tend to be noncompliant."

Most of us have enough things we must do in our lives. Living up to an "exercise prescription" quickly falls to the bottom of our lists. If our goal is to lose weight and that doesn't happen quickly, many decide to go back to "driving for pleasure."

Yet I'm the first to suggest that now is as good a time as any to consider increasing your level of physical activity. Finding something you like to do is the key. Like most women, the main reason I am physically active is not because it prolongs life, but because it makes every day more enjoyable.

# *Thankfully, Mom Encouraged Outdoor Play*

W HAT MAKES A GOOD MOTHER? DO MOMS EVER FEEL THEY know enough? Was it much easier to raise children fifty years ago?

Things certainly have changed. When I was growing up, most mothers stayed home. Life seemed easier. Women talked to their families or friends for guidance on how to raise children. Yet I suspect my mother would have attended the conference sponsored by the Minnesota Smith College Alumnae entitled, "Full Esteem Ahead! Preparing Our Daughters for Life in the 21st Century."

Why? Because my self-esteem dropped precipitously when I was a teenager. It was sometimes hard for my mom and me to talk. At this conference, mothers and daughters had a chance to share experiences, an activity that helped make their problems seem more universal. I was glad one session was directed toward physical activity and its effect on self-confidence.

To what extent do mothers influence their daughters to be physically active? Some of my best memories of growing up are connected with the physical activities I  shared with my mom. My brother recently had our old 16mm movies put on videotape for my dad's eightieth birthday. They confirmed my memories that ours was an active childhood.

There were shots of running through the sprinkler, of

acrobatics performed for the circus we organized in the empty lot. There were shots of me learning to ride my first two-wheeled bike. My Mom had not received her first bike until she was thirteen, and she wanted us to taste the freedom it offered at a younger age.

Like most women of her era, my mom left the workforce as soon as she married. I have fond memories of frequent walks with her to explore the Mississippi River. When I was older, my friends and I explored the neighborhood on our bikes. My mom encouraged adventure and independence. She believed playing outside made you strong and resilient.

She had some formidable opposition at times. When I was in the sixth grade, she walked to school to try to convince our gym teacher that girls should have some time on the softball diamond, too. She did not succeed.

Today, a whole body of research documents that girls' self-esteem and confidence often suffer during adolescence. Experts inform moms about the link between physical activity, competence and confidence.

My mom just used her best instincts. She didn't try to dissuade me from reading, but she made sure I also challenged myself physically. Some of the few memories I have of feeling competent during my teen years are of being at Girl Scout camp. There it didn't matter if I was a bookworm and fat; I was a good swimmer, a strong canoeist and could carry a heavy pack.

I learned from my mom that going on a bike ride could help me heal disappointments and feel better about myself.

My mom died nine years ago, before I adequately thanked her for believing in me and encouraging me always to be on the lookout for adventure. I don't know if I ever told her she was my hero. She would have been embarrassed and shrugged it off. She also would have been pleased.

# Fathers Play a Key Role in Girls Athletics

S HOW ME A MAN WITH A DAUGHTER, AND I KNOW I HAVE a very good chance of interesting him in women's sports. Men become interested in opportunities for girls because of a mother or spouse, but it's their daughters who seem to make the biggest difference.

"My daughter is just as skilled as her brothers," said a recent caller to the Women's Sports Foundation, which promotes sports for girls and women. "I'm appalled that there are so few opportunities for her." While the situation has improved for the elite athlete since the passing of Title IX in 1972, many girls still find limited chances to learn and play.

That's where dads can make a real difference. The 1995 Melpomene Institute study on girls who play high school hockey found that dads who had played hockey were important sources of encouragement for their daughters.

It's not only competitive athletes who need a dad's support. Many women of all ages who consider themselves recreational participants say their dads play a key role.

My friend Barb Andersen recalls a special incident. "I was thirteen in 1936," Barb said. "It was in the middle of the Depression. My stepfather took me out to buy a baseball glove so I could play in the city league. My mom's first question was, 'How much did it cost?' My dad's response was immediate: 'This is one time we don't worry about the money; she needs a good glove.'"

Barb also remembers that young men in her neighborhood played ball and taught all the kids how to play. "They didn't single out boys," she said. "We all served a kind of baseball apprenticeship; by the end I had earned my place on the field. I remember that time very fondly. The confidence I gained has made a difference in my life."

Another friend, Sally Patterson, remembers that her family's attitude toward females and sports was different from that of other families she knew. Her family went skiing and canoeing and played tennis together.

"My mother was game to do anything," Sally said. "My father fully expected my mother and his three daughters to participate in every activity that he did; in the late 1940s that was unusual."

Barb and Sally grew up before Title IX gave girls the opportunity to participate at higher levels. Attitudes have changed. Men can see girls and women excelling in a wide variety of sports. Because many dads have personal knowledge of the positive value of sports, they often play a critical role in getting daughters to participate.

Shestin and Kajsa Larson, sisters ages ten and fifteen, give their dad a lot of credit for their sports participation. Kajsa, who concentrates on volleyball and track, said, "He encourages me. He always lets me know how proud and happy he is that I'm in sports." Shestin added that her dad "tells me if I'm doing a good job and where I can improve."

Their dad, Dan Larson, said, "It's an important part of a girl's life. I think I should be there to encourage and support them. It's fun for me to see how much they learn from sports."

A dad showing interest in his daughter's physical abilities and giving her encouragement and applause can make a big difference.

# *Exercise During Pregnancy: How Much Is Okay?*

D OES RUNNING A TWENTY-SIX-MILE MARATHON ONE WEEK and completing sixty-three miles during a twenty-four-hour running event the next weekend sound challenging to you? That's what Sue Olsen of Burnsville, Minnesota, did. She received all kinds of media attention because she also happened to be eight and three-quarters months pregnant.

I think it's time to put Olsen's decision in perspective.

Athletic women and the physicians who treat them concurred that Olsen was not a typical runner. Her level of training and conditioning was extraordinary. Her long-distance running late in pregnancy was not harmful. Neither should it be seen as an ideal or something others should strive to do.

What is realistic for most women?

Until the last one hundred years or so, most women were forced by circumstance to exercise during pregnancy. Women often worked in the fields or stood at laborious factory jobs until the day of delivery. In the late 1800s, attitudes changed. If you could afford to take time off work during pregnancy, you did. Women were cautioned to limit physical activity.

That attitude persisted. When my mother was pregnant in the early 1940s, physical activity was discouraged. Even in 1967, some people were surprised or critical when I continued to ride my bike while pregnant.

In 1982, Melpomene Institute conducted its first study of exercise and pregnancy. It was designed in response to the many phone calls and letters we received asking what was safe and sensible. Many physicians still actively discouraged physical activity. Those who didn't often admitted they were frustrated by the lack of research.

In 1986, the American College of Obstetrics and Gynecology issued guidelines that raised the ire of many women who had decided to exercise during pregnancy. The reason? The guidelines seemed unnecessarily restrictive. The 1994 guidelines issued by the organization were more lenient and realistic.

That reflects a change in medical advice, which has become more supportive of physical activity during pregnancy. The first concern of pregnant women is safety, but they continue to receive conflicting messages.

"All of a sudden, people are questioning my decision to continue to be physically active," said Maren Patterson, when she was five months pregnant. "That seems contradictory, since I've been told all my life that physical activity is a health benefit. More important, it's one of the things I do for fun. It makes me feel good about myself and my body."

One participant in Melpomene's study said, "The first time I wanted to prove it was possible, so I prided myself on running right up to the delivery date. This time, I'm still physically active, because that's my lifestyle, but I'm walking and swimming in my last months."

Susan Cushman, a Minneapolis obstetrician who ran during her pregnancy twelve years ago, encourages her patients to be physically active during pregnancy. She also reminds them they have absolutely nothing to prove during pregnancy. "I encourage them to be boringly average. That's when the pregnancy is most likely to be normal," she said.

It's all about what's good and healthy for both mother and baby.

# *War on Fat Makes an Enemy of Good Food*

I USED TO BE VERY AWARE OF THE CALORIC CONTENT OF foods. I worried if I gained a pound or two. I weighed myself at least once a day. Unfortunately, I was not unique.

I'm not talking about eating disorders but about disordered eating, which is a problem for many women. Physically active women are not immune from being preoccupied with food. Many have decided to exercise as a means to become thinner.

Nancy Clark, a registered dietitian and director of nutrition services at Sportsmedicine Brookline in the Boston area, wrote in the March 1995 issue of *The Physician and Sportsmedicine,* "Thousands of today's weight conscious athletes have become afraid of dietary fat. They fear that if a gram of fat crosses their lips, it will turn into pounds of fat on their hips. They avoid eating fat-containing foods — from bran muffins to birthday cakes — and select a limited diet that commonly includes bagels, fruit, vegetables, plain pasta, baked potatoes, pretzels, rice cakes, fat-free cookies and frozen yogurt."

Many also feel guilty if they "cheat" and eat some ice cream or a potato chip.

In the search to be healthy, many women and some men have gone too far. Clark explains that some fat is necessary in the diet. It's a vital nutrient that supplies the body with essential fatty acids. We're well aware that it adds a flavor to foods that's hard to match. Fat also is digested more slowly than protein or carbohydrates and therefore satisfies your hunger longer.

"Fat avoiders may end up with food obsessions and other nutrition concerns. These nibbles add calories — regardless if the calories are from a fat-free bagel, pretzel or apple, or if they are from chocolate chip cookies," Clark wrote.

Many American women seem to have forgotten how to enjoy food. I never fit that description, but as a fat kid, I learned that some foods had more calories and should be avoided. For years, I ate salads and healthy non-fattening foods in the search for thinness. I was successful, if success can be measured by having a thinner body.

I also decided it was not worth the effort. The turning point for me was living in Tunisia, where a focal point of the day was eating meals. I learned the pleasure of a two-hour dinner, with delicious food and stimulating conversation. I once again appreciated the wonderful variety and taste of many foods, including those I had kept out of my diet for years.

Most Tunisians seem unaware of calories. They regard food as a source of both fuel and pleasure. I realized my own attitudes had shifted significantly after I'd returned home. I was having lunch with a friend. We both ordered salads. She was amazed when I had two slices of the delicious crusty bread.

"I never eat bread," she said. "It's too fattening." I didn't say anything then because I didn't want to spoil our lunch or our friendship with a discussion about my decision to stop feeling guilty for enjoying food.

Clark wrote, "Your health and sanity will be better off if you give yourself permission to freely eat and enjoy appropriate amounts of fatty food. Remember, eating is not a moral issue. You are not bad if you eat fat. Eating should be one of life's pleasures, not a source of guilt."

Summer is a great time to enjoy food. Combine it with regular physical activity, and you'll be healthier no matter what your size.

# Gardening Yields Health and Exercise Benefits

T HIS SUMMER I'VE SCANNED THE PAPER LOOKING FOR
announcements of garden tours. I haven't been disappointed and have spent several weekends looking at other peoples'
gardens. I go because I love to see beautiful gardens and because
I'm always looking for new ideas for mine.

When I was a kid, I wondered how my aunt could spend
so much time in her garden. Now I understand. There is something soothing and addicting about seeing a garden grow. If
you're an amateur, as I am, the results aren't always predictable.
Experienced gardeners tell me good gardens take long-term
planning. Like many who are new to the activity, I'm interested
in learning.

Obviously, I'm not the only recent convert. Sales for
gardening activities jumped more than 15 percent in 1994, according to a survey conducted for the National Gardening Association by the Gallup organization.

The National Gardening Association is an educational
organization dedicated to community improvement through gardening. It publishes a how-to magazine that has 250,000 sub-
scribers, establishes school programs that use gardening to teach
science concepts and operates the on-line gardening forum on
CompuServe.

The survey indicates that in 1994, three out of four

households, numbering seventy-two million people, participated in lawn and garden activities. I'm not particularly pleased that the majority of the money spent was on lawn care ($8 billion dollars). As a matter of fact, I just read about a product called "No mow, no mo," a specially designed blend of low-growing turf grasses. The developers say you can mow once a month if you're compulsive, but that mowing really isn't necessary. Cutting down on lawn care sounds like a good investment to me.

I feel quite differently about flower and vegetable gardens. The small garden I started ten years ago has grown each year. I spend many happy hours planting and weeding.

The July/August 1995 issue of *Health* magazine supports the idea that gardening is not only good for the soul but benefits the body as well. Gardening receives a lot of attention in an article titled "Dynamic Duos." The idea is that gardening offers a variety of activities to keep you moving. It's also true that most of us are better off combining several methods of exercise. Until recently, gardening wasn't included on those lists.

Many women who garden might be happy to realize they are reaping the benefits of physical activity. *Health* lists gardening as one of the top five "easiest to start," as well as one of the best to provide an upper body workout. It pairs gardening with bicycling and aerobic dance as good ways to get a total body workout.

According to *Health,* "Gardening works up a sweat, makes an hour pass as quickly as a minute and leaves you with a feeling of accomplishment. . . . Gardening challenges the body differently. Raking, weeding, hauling and bagging are nature's weight training, toning your biceps, triceps, back, shoulders, legs and rump."

The only time I think about those body parts in relation to gardening is the morning after a major weeding, when I wake up with all kinds of new aches and pains. Still, the pleasure I gain from watching my gardens grow makes the effort worth it.

# Elderhostel Trips Offer Adventure and Education

F IFTEEN YEARS AGO, WHEN I WORKED AT THE UNIVERSITY of Minnesota, my office was next to the Elderhostel offices, whose trips seemed wonderful. I recommended them to my parents and their friends.

It's hard to believe I am now eligible for their offerings. In 1994, Elderhostel decided to lower the age limit to 55. Carol Daly, state director of Minnesota Elderhostel, said the decision was a good one. "People are retiring earlier, and the demand was there," she said. In 1994, twenty-nine thousand people enrolled.

You don't have to be retired to participate in Elderhostel's many offerings. Programs are offered year-round by a network of nearly two thousand educational and cultural institutions. Most programs in the United States and Canada are one week in length; overseas offerings last two to four weeks. Fees are very reasonable: in 1995, the average cost for a week in the United States was $340. Partial scholarships are also available.

When the program was founded in 1975, the emphasis was on educational enrichment. While all offerings consist of some course work, there are no homework assignments, exams or grades. Based on the latest survey, distributed in 1989, 61 percent of Elderhostel participants were female; 50 percent were seventy or older and 70 percent were married.

Yet some of the program's biggest boosters are widows.

"It's a great opportunity to do really exciting things that I probably wouldn't do on my own," said my friend Yvonne Wagner. She started taking one big trip a year almost twenty years ago. Now eighty-three years old, Yvonne said she has decided all her trips will be through the Elderhostel program. "I want to keep learning as well as seeing new places," she said. "Nobody provides the opportunity for that better than Elderhostel."

Over the years, programs that incorporate hiking, canoeing and outdoor adventures have been given more emphasis. The trips are very popular. The current Minnesota list includes a course entitled "Wilderness Adventure: Canoeing in the Boundary Waters Canoe Area." According to the catalogue, participants will "experience the Boundary Waters Canoe Area wilderness as the early adventurers did, firsthand. Explore the land and lakes for wildflowers, nesting birds and animals of the boreal forest. Live a rugged lifestyle canoeing to primitive campsites."

Believe it or not, a lot of sixty- and seventy-year-old women are clamoring for the opportunity.

Another change that appeals to many is Elderhostel's trips for grandparents and grandchildren. A program called "The Grand Adventure: Exploring Nature with Your Grandchildren," offered twice in late August, filled quickly. Activities included tracking animals, banding birds and trying a ropes course and rock-climbing wall. Grandchildren must be between the ages of eight and twelve, and up to two children per grandparent are allowed.

Jan and Charlie Lloyd have been to four intergenerational offerings. The Lloyds' trips have included a South Dakota Black Hills wagon train, marine biology in Texas and the Wolf Ridge Environmental Learning Center in Finland, Minnesota.

"We love to do these trips because of the very special time we can spend with our grandchildren," Jan Lloyd said.

For more information, call the Elderhostel national office at (617) 426-8056. In addition, most local libraries carry the Elderhostel catalogue, which describes all of the programs.

# Level
# Playing
# Fields

# *More Women Are Teeing Off*

M Y DAD, ALMOST EIGHTY, STILL PLAYS AN IMPRESSIVE GAME of golf three times a week. Golf is an important part of his social life. Historically, that's been true for many men but not for many women.

One reason is that the world of golf has not been particularly hospitable to women. Many states allow clubs to restrict the times and hours when women can play. That was true in Minnesota until 1986, when a law was passed that sharply increased the taxes of private clubs if they continued to discriminate against women golfers.

At first, the law was vigorously opposed by many men. They were afraid that giving women equal access would significantly limit their privileged position. Prior to passage of the Minnesota law, women were unable to get Saturday or Sunday morning tee times. Many courses gave preferential treatment to men during the week as well.

The presumption was that women were free to golf mid-week and mid-day. Women argued that times had changed. Most women now also have schedules that preclude playing golf during the week.

Increased opportunities have increased the number of women golfers. It is estimated that nearly five million women played golf in 1988; numbers swelled to five and one-half million in 1990 and just over six million in 1991.

Many business women report they begin playing golf because it is smart or even necessary for career advancement. It is estimated that half of women golfers are managers, professionals or administrators.

Women who regard golf as a way of enhancing their jobs are also likely to take lessons and treat the game seriously. "It doesn't make sense to go golfing with the guys and feel like you're the worst player," one woman golfer said.

To meet the growing demand, there are now more than a dozen schools nationwide with programs tailored to women. The Ladies Professional Golf Association holds golf clinics in ten cities. The executive women's golf league, founded two and one-half years ago, now has sixty chapters and thirty-five hundred members.

As women become more serious about the game, they look for ways to improve. Traditional golf magazines are still very male-oriented. It's little wonder then that *Golf for Women,* first published in August 1988, has found a ready market. Current circulation is three hundred thousand and growing quickly. Most of the articles are related to golf technique, equipment and descriptions of outstanding courses. However, articles describing how to enter tournaments and how to encourage kids to start golfing at an early age suggest the range of interests of readers.

Many other women take up golf because it sounds like fun. "I was getting tired of biking. I looked for something that was social but challenging," one woman said.

Another golfer said, "As a kid I didn't have the chance to try golf. But I'm coordinated and a quick learner. I'm expecting to be a good golfer."

Many women are looking for a sport they can continue playing as they age. Like my dad, they're finding golf makes growing old a lot more fun.

# A River Runs through It for Both Genders

I HOOKED SOMETHING BIG FLY-FISHING LAST WEEK. UNfortunately, it was my leg. That's the kind of thing some people expect of women.

My introduction to fly-fishing was not auspicious. We hired a guide, but he paid much more attention to my husband and son than to me. We were in Utah, where attitudes about women are notoriously chauvinistic. The men with me received excellent instruction; I watched from my place downstream.

After an hour or so, the guide wandered down to me, hooked a fish with ease and helped me land it. He sighed in relief, "You've caught your fish for the day. I was afraid you'd spoil my record." His mission of having me "catch" a fish accomplished, he disappeared to attend to the men, leaving me as ignorant as ever.

The scene almost repeated itself a year later during a trip I made to speak at a Nike conference in the same state. This time, a few more women were fly-fishing with me, but all the guides tried to be assigned to the one group that was all male.

Our group consisted of a twenty-three-year-old woman, a thirty-five-year-old man and me. In this case, the instructor seemed more concerned about my age than my gender. When I managed to climb down a steep cliff without injury, he began to treat us more equally. I learned more about the skill required to fly-fish that day, although the instructor still felt compelled to "help" rather than teach. Later, he told the other guides with pride that he had helped the "old lady" in his group land the biggest fish of the day.

It was therefore a delightful surprise when I went fly-fishing in Idaho with a guide who believed older women could be good at the sport. He told me that one of his favorite students was an eighty-nine-year-old woman who fished with him regularly.

Intrigued, I interviewed Clara Spiegel by phone at her home in Ketchum, Idaho. Her sparkling voice was full of zest when she told me she'd started fly-fishing in 1939. She admitted to slowing down a little with age. To Clara, that means resting a day between fishing expeditions. She credits guide Richard Winkler with making fishing a continuing adventure.

A woman who loves the outdoors, Clara started riding horses at five and expects to be back on a horse next spring after recuperating from surgery. But, she says, "Fly-fishing is the most hypnotic thing I've ever done. No matter what my problems, I lose them on the river."

Clara reminded me that if I want to become a good fly-fisher, I need to think like a fish.

Those two aspects of fly-fishing — the hypnotic and the intellectual — have attracted men to the sport for years. But, even though it has not been well known, women have participated, too.

One of the earliest books describing fly-fishing was authored by Dame Juliana Berners, a fifteenth-century prioress. In 1932, women serious about fly-fishing chose her as the patron saint of the club they created exclusively for women anglers.

More women are sure to take up the sport as they learn the joy of standing in a beautiful stream trying to outwit a fish. Like Clara, many will discover that fly-fishing knows no age limits. When Clara goes to Yellowstone again, the fish better be smart!

# Cross-Country Skiing Is a Good Lifelong Sport

I WAS ONE OF THOSE PEOPLE LONGING FOR SNOW. IT WAS great to bike on Thanksgiving Day, but I was ready to get out my cross-country skis.

I was not alone. The Monday after the season's first snow, I was at Como golf course with fifty others, trying to make our own tracks through the fluffy snow. There were several high-school students and some kids who obviously were trying skis for the first time. I saw a woman with two young kids who were alternately laughing and complaining.

My spouse and I introduced each of our kids to cross-country skiing when they were three. Ahvo Taipale, local expert and promoter of cross-country skiing, told me he again is seeing more families out in all the city and county parks. He explained, "In the 1980s, when skating skis became the rage, many skiers dropped out."

I almost quit, too. After years of plowing through the snow in the traditional manner, I felt foolish when everyone whizzed past me on the trail. But I had someone who encouraged me to try new equipment and techniques. Our son Reid had become a good cross-country skier. In 1985, he joined the St. Paul Central High School team. Only seven students tried out even though suburban schools, notably Hastings and Stillwater, were attracting large numbers.

In the four years Reid was at Central, things changed. Good coaching by Paul Virgin and personal dedication earned several individuals the chance to compete in the state meet. Competing in that event was the highlight of Reid's year and encouraged him to continue to excel in a Division I college program.

Coach Virgin's philosophy is one I applaud. He makes it clear you don't need to race to come out for the sport. He wants to introduce as many kids as possible to an activity they can enjoy for a lifetime.

Everybody who comes out is allowed to ski at every meet during the season. That's quite different from most competitive sports, in which only the best get a chance.

I recently attended one of the big meets. The sight was amazing and inspiring. More than two hundred fifty kids were there, cheered on by a huge crowd of parents.

A cheering crowd is one of the highlights of competition. I didn't have a chance to compete as a kid; cross-country skiing gives me that opportunity now. Even if I'm at the back of the pack, there's someone telling me I'm looking good.

That encourages me to continue to improve. Reid is still my best teacher, but I got a jump start on technique by attending one of the holiday camps conducted by Taipale.

The North Star Ski Touring Club has also provided valuable service for the past twenty-eight years. One of the benefits of club membership is a subscription to *Loype,* a newsletter full of information for both the novice and expert skier. The winter calendar enclosed in the November edition lists trips, dinners and races. The Minnesota Youth Ski League, now three years old, offers lessons and encouragement for kids four to fifteen.

If you need a new winter sport, cross-country skiing has much to offer.

# Women's Pro Softball Steps to the Plate

I N 1988, JANE COWLES VISITED HER FORMER COLLEGE fastpitch coach in San Diego. Their dream of creating a professional league will be realized this summer. Significant long-term planning, including a sound investment plan, makes the odds for success high.

Women's Professional Fastpitch (WPF) will provide a rare opportunity for women to participate in a professional sport. Jane's vision is that the players will earn enough to make it a full-time job. Her goals are to pay equitably and create a league that has staying power.

Women have always played softball. It's the most popular recreational sport in America, with more than forty million people of all ages playing the game each year. More than seven million girls between the ages of seven and seventeen play softball.

The timing for the new league is right. In 1994, fastpitch softball registered the biggest gain in girls high school athletic programs. Organizers of the new league estimate the growing pool of talented players includes two hundred fifty thousand high-school varsity and twenty-eight thousand college athletes. Skill levels also have risen dramatically. Last year two top awards, the NCAA Honda Broderick Cup award and the Women's Sports Foundation Team Sportswoman of the Year, went to fastpitch players.

Further, fastpitch will be a medal sport at the 1996 Olympics in Atlanta, adding credibility and recognition. Team USA has dominated international competition and is predicted to win the gold.

Organizers of WPF have been working to make changes in the game so it will appeal to a wider audience. Traditional fastpitch has emphasized a dominating pitcher, with games characterized by many strikeouts and low scores. While fans may appreciate the skill involved, it's not very exciting to watch.

To increase the action, WPF has adopted larger field dimensions and a smaller, livelier ball. The result: a game that generates more hits and base running. The concept has been tested dozens of times with collegiate and elite amateur players. The response has been enthusiastic.

Before moving ahead with plans for WPF, the organizers reviewed the data gathered by Team Research Foundation to examine why earlier women's pro sports leagues had failed. The major reasons were location, lack of expert sport management, poor promotion and inadequate financial backing.

WPF teams will be located in mid-sized Midwestern cities with populations of at least one hundred thousand who are not the home for other professional sports teams. Locating teams in adjoining states means teams can travel by bus, a major cost saving. The league-owned teams will be well financed through investors and professionally managed.

The Midwest has been selected as the testing ground because of its long history of softball participation. The region also has demonstrated strong support for women's athletics. Team tryouts for the 1995 WPF tour will be announced within the next month. Twelve to eighteen games are being scheduled at minor league baseball stadiums.

The first full season is scheduled for 1996, with six teams playing a seventy-game season. I predict the stands will be filled. The chance to play professional sports is a dream for many girls and women. The opportunity is long overdue.

# Girls Take Slap Shots into History

H ISTORY WILL BE MADE THIS WEEKEND WHEN THE FIRST
girls state high school hockey tournament in the nation is
held at Aldrich Arena in St. Paul, Minnesota.

The Minnesota State High School League decided in
1994 to include girls hockey as an official sport. Twenty-four
teams were needed for the league to sponsor a tournament; that
number was reached by summer's end.

Those who know hockey are not surprised at the boom-
ing interest in the sport. Minnesota has a history of good hockey
at the club level for girls and women. But longtime club hockey
players like Emily Sherman are excited that girls hockey finally is
an official high school sport.

"It gives girls a real boost to have a state tournament,"
Sherman said. "We're already seeing huge growth in participation by younger girls. Last year we had thirteen teams for girls
eight to twelve. This year there are fifty teams in the metro area."

These girls, just like their brothers who start playing
hockey at a young age, will have better skills when they reach
high school. Thousands of boys play hockey, so it's tough for a
boy to make the varsity squad. Girls who have tried to play on
boys teams have had to be very good. When Libby Witchger
made the 1990 Wayzata team, she was the only girl.

It's clear from research being conducted at Melpomene

Institute that many girls have been waiting for the opportunity. Many became interested in hockey because a father or brother played. Because there have been so few women hockey players who have received media attention, most of their role models are men.

Some of those men are very supportive; others, particularly boy hockey players, are sometimes less than enthusiastic. A sample of some of the typical comments girls said they'd heard from boys: "Girls can't skate; they're sloppy!" "Girls can't play a guys' sport." "It's a waste of money to let girls play." "Girls games are stupid; I'd never go to one!" "Girls are taking our ice time."

Some of the comments are justified. The caliber of play this season is spotty. The experience level varies greatly from player to player. But ask the girls how they feel, and they are enthusiastic about playing on a girls team. One player said, "When I played with boys, they made fun of me, even if I was good." Another said, "It's more fun because the guys always thought they were better than me."

The girls are determined to improve their skills. When asked what they would like to accomplish in the first season, only a few mentioned winning. Instead, the girls talked about improving their stick handling or slap shot, scoring a goal. Others hoped to build a good team. One girl summed it up: "Win some games, learn a lot, get the program grounded."

The tournament this weekend will prove that girls hockey at the high school level has arrived. A new group of women is reading the sports pages to see how their favorite team fared. The lopsided scores will be less common in 1996.

Many of those in attendance will be girls whose teams did not make the cut. They'll be there because they want to see good hockey. They realize the addition of hockey as an official high school sport is giving them more equal treatment.

"I'm honored and proud to be playing hockey," a player said.

# Mighty Mary *Shows Women Can Compete*

Y OU COULD FIND MEDIA COVERAGE OF WOMEN IN SPORTS every day. The reason? *Mighty Mary* was part of the America's Cup. The America's Cup was going to be covered; it's part of the stuff that makes up the sports pages. The fact that there was an all-women's boat probably increased the coverage.

On January 13, 1995, the *New York Times* reported, "It was a momentous day in the America's Cup, and a milestone for sport in general. Although one race does not a victory make in the America's Cup, in the opening match today of the Citizen Cup defender trials, the unseasoned *America* women's team defeated a highly touted male *Stars and Stripes* crew by one minute, nine seconds.

"More important, *America* won the first race in what is thought to be the first sporting competition between a women's team and a men's team."

The chance to compete on the America's Cup team obviously appealed to many women. The final crew was chosen from six hundred fifty applicants. The crew included three Olympic medalists, three former yachtswomen of the year, one aerospace engineer, two world class weightlifters and a former American Gladiator.

The women had only eight months to train. They sailed on the older *America* before receiving *Mighty Mary,* their new super boat, in the fourth round. Some say the boat is the critical factor. It evens the odds. Yet at that juncture, Bill Koch, the *America* team benefactor, was quoted as saying: "They've shown that they have the strength, and they have the technique. What's left is strictly in their heads. Can they really compete against men? Can they really cut it?"

The skills needed to adapt to changing situations, one of the factors that makes the America's Cup so exciting to follow, were present. It's not just brute strength, but the ability to adapt, cooperate and improvise as a crew that is needed to win. But one critical factor may have been missing. Crew member Anna Seaton Huntington wrote that from the outset, "Koch and his associates decided he and the all-male coaching staff would have control over the team." There was no female captain on board for everyone to turn to for the final word.

Four weeks after publicly challenging the women, Koch seemed to answer his own question in the negative. On March 20, David Dellenbaugh replaced J.J. Isler as tactician and assumed a leadership role. The switch was made in haste and apparently without the knowledge of more than a handful of the crew.

Two weeks after *Mighty Mary* lost to *Stars and Stripes'* Dennis Conner, Huntington wrestled with her feelings. She wrote, "One thing is clear: We know we scared the heck out of Conner in that last race. Even though he ended up winning, we led for five of the six legs, and there is no way after four months of trading races that he or anyone else can say that women don't belong out on the race course."

I was disappointed at the loss. I wonder if the results might have been different if the women had had more responsibility and less advice from men. Yet I also believe Huntington was right when she concluded the *America* crew provided a "crucial, but small, first step along the way to change."

# *Masters Runners Share Their Stories*

MASTER'S WOMEN ARE COMING INTO THEIR OWN. WHAT IS a master? That depends on your sport. In running you need to be forty.

I was in New York City recently to speak at a Master's Clinic held in conjunction with the Advil Mini-Marathon. The race, a ten-kilometer run through Central Park, is now twenty-four years old. It's the premier women's race in the country, routinely drawing more than eight thousand participants.

This is the first year they have held a master's clinic. Advil and the New York Road Runners Club, sponsors of the event, were smart. They knew there was a huge audience of women waiting to have their needs addressed.

Four hundred women attended. Many had never tried racing before, yet they seemed excited to give it a try. For some, admitting they were forty was difficult. Moderator Sharon Barbano told her own story of limiting her horizons after Mikey, the sixteen-year-old in her biking group, asked everyone to reveal their ages. It turned out Barbano, at forty-two, was eight or more years older than everyone else.

"Instead of riding at the front of the pack where I often rode before I publicly admitted my age, I found myself at the back," Barbano said. "I became more cautious. While my skill level was the same, I started to believe I should 'act my age.' Then one day in a race I found myself just behind Mikey. Suddenly I realized that I belonged at the front. I passed Mikey with ease. My age didn't matter. What mattered was attitude."

Barbano's story struck a chord. Yet women had concerns that went beyond attitude. Growing older makes some women particularly self-conscious about their appearance. One woman asked, "Are there any really lightweight tights that I can wear in the summer? I have spider marks on my legs, and I won't show them in public." Another woman's husband had discouraged her because he said running at her age would lead to sagging breasts.

Many of the questions were related to health. Some wondered about the relationship between menopause and running. One forty-five-year-old woman asked what I knew about continuing to run during pregnancy. She surmised, correctly, that there wasn't a lot of information available to her.

One of the impressive elements of the seminar was that women who had been strangers began to share information. Many of the more seasoned runners talked of the power their sport provided. "I diminish some of the stereotypes of aging," one woman said. "That improves my self-image and means I tackle things on the job that seemed impossible. One of the strengths of an all-women's event is that women are less fearful to give it a try."

The master's division continues to grow as women over forty are finding strength and pleasure in testing their bodies. "I may be getting slower," said Mary Lou Carlson, who has set many age-group records, "but I'll never stop racing. It's changed my life, and I want to encourage others. It can do the same for them."

# First Triathlon Was a Comedy of Errors

M Y FIRST ENCOUNTER WITH TRIATHLONS WAS FAIRLY BEnign. That's because I decided the way to approach this sport, which combines swimming, biking and running, was as a member of a team.

I was the designated swimmer. The swim went well. As I waited for the rest of my team to bike and run, I enjoyed the chance to relax and visit. I didn't really observe how tired some of the competitors looked at the end.

The next year, I decided it was time to try a full triathlon. This "long" triathlon included a three-quarter mile swim, twenty-four-mile bike ride and five-mile run. I figured I was in good shape from running so I did little advance preparation.

To arrive in time for the 7:00 A.M. start, I needed to bail out of bed at 5:30. I had arranged to meet a friend before the race to pick up my race number as well as borrow an approved bike helmet.

I arrived on time, but five minutes before the race, my friend was nowhere to be seen. Just as people were lining up to enter the water, we spotted each other. I completed my equipment inventory just moments before the race began.

The swim was okay. The lake was shallow in the middle, so I could take a short rest by walking. A year ago, I swam twice as far and was less tired. I suspect this time I was worried about what waited ahead.

At the transition area, serious triathletes have pails of water to wash their sandy feet. They have shoes lined up so they don't waste time between events.

Near-sighted people have other priorities. My equipment included a cereal bowl of water, my contact lens wetting solution, a washrag and a mirror. I had trouble inserting my contacts immediately after emerging from the water — they swam around my eyes instead of centering. When my contacts were in place, I shoved on my shorts, both legs in one on the first try, then had trouble hooking the strap on my helmet.

A full five minutes after completing the swim, I roared out of the transition area and entered the biking part of the race.

One of my pre-race fears was that I would crash on my bike. However, when you are in the oldest age group, swim only moderately well and take a five-minute break getting your act together between the swim and bike, there is little traffic on the race course.

The first three miles were relatively flat and fun. However, on the first hill I noticed a problem. I struggled with my gears and realized I couldn't shift. The night before I had broken a sensible rule: Know your equipment and make no changes prior to a race.

I'd broken that rule when I added a water bottle to my bike frame and inadvertently taped the cable down. That eliminated any possibility of shifting gears. Although I was initially annoyed, I discovered my one-speed bike ride was okay. It also provided humor for others as I went slowly uphill and rapidly downhill.

When the biking event was over, I wished the run were shorter than five miles. However, I had physiological and mental edges because I'm basically a runner. But I was still a very tired finisher.

The fatigue was short-lived, though, and the challenge was more fun than running a race. So each summer I enter one or two triathlons. They are always an adventure.

# *Triathletes Are Enjoying Life Off the Couch*

I WAS VISITING MY FRIEND BETH GRUBER WHEN I NOTICED the sign on the bulletin board for the Becketwood Triathlon. I was interested immediately because Becketwood is a cooperative with a minimum age requirement of fifty-five.

"Work Up an Appetite for the Independence Day Buffet," read the announcement. The activities were not the same as a usual triathlon. Instead, there was golf at 2:00, croquet at 3:00 and horseshoes at 4:00.

When I was a kid, Beth had been my Girl Scout leader. She taught me many things, but she didn't strike me as being particularly athletic.

A few years before my recent visit, Beth had purchased her own putter for a golf tournament at Becketwood. She won third prize in a hotly contested series of matches. The plaque hangs in a prominent place in her entryway.

But she was not a contestant this year. She's recovering from hip replacement surgery, and her physical activity challenge now consists of getting from her apartment to the elevator. She's timing herself so she can chart her progress.

But many of her friends were at the triathlon, even though the weather was not ideal. The number of participants was lower than it would have been if the sun had been shining, and spectators carried umbrellas. On the golf course, an eighteen-hole putting green, more men than women were participants, even though the ratio of women to men at Becketwood is more than two to one. "Golf is something many men have done all their lives," said one participant. "A lot of us women are just beginning in our seventies and eighties."

After twenty-seven holes, four people were tied. Jessie Howell, the only woman among them, had several impressive putts. As we walked to the croquet field together, she told me she hadn't played much golf before. "I played basketball in junior high school, and we liked to go hiking, but girls didn't play golf in the early 1930s," she said.

The low-key nature of the event was evident, as several people admitted they had never even played croquet before. Others had some experience but weren't at all sure about the rules. Some were serious and competitive, while others laughed at their lack of skill. Midway during the event, it began to rain harder, and about half of the participants headed for shelter.

The six who stuck it out for the final event tossed horseshoes. Four used the regular horseshoes; two opted for new lightweight ones.

The women and men I saw defied stereotypes of aging. Some used walkers, and a few observed from their wheelchairs, yet the overall impression I got was one of health and vitality. Some naysayers insist that it's almost impossible to get adults who have been sedentary to exercise in their later years. But concentrating on the social aspects of physical activity and making it fun obviously have encouraged many seniors at Becketwood to get off the couch. The benefits, both psychological and physical, are easy to see.

Beth Gruber had to borrow a club when she first headed out to the putting green. "Everyone told me it was fun, that I should try it. This is a friendly place, so I just joined in," she said.

# *Rent a Bike, Find a Guide, Try a Trail*

Y OU CAN TELL YOU'RE GETTING OLDER, OR MAYBE JUST wiser with age, when you decide a mountain bike trail is just too difficult.

My spouse and I were in Colorado recently. We returned to a bed-and-breakfast in Breckenridge known for its hot tub and huge breakfasts. The owners remembered us because on our first visit we'd dashed out to run a five-kilometer race before eating. They'd wondered how we lowlanders would do. We survived, but it was the toughest race I have ever run in my life. We spent the rest of our time mountain biking with our daughter, Wendy. It was a much better way to get our exercise.

I first learned to bike when I was a kid. In recent years, I've moved from my trusty and reliable three-speed to a twelve-speed with racing handlebars. We ride the hills of Wisconsin almost every weekend. But that is not at all the same as biking on real mountain trails.

Our son Reid, who was living in Park City, Utah, introduced us to mountain biking. He probably overestimated our abilities, but he was careful not to get us in real trouble.

At first the path was a double track that could be used by four-wheeled vehicles. Soon, however, it turned into a single track that wound its way up a mountain. Reid, a skilled athlete and rider, had to pause frequently so we could catch up. I found myself walking on occasion; I also discovered the amazing ability of the bike to jump over rocks and be very maneuverable.

Good mountain bikes are constructed to have more stability than racing or street bikes. They have an oversized frame and tubing to handle the stress of off-road riding. The wheels are smaller in diameter; the wider, knobby tires absorb shock and provide more friction for climbing and cornering. For that reason, they handle very well on mountain trails. They are much slower than other bikes on paved trails.

Nonetheless, Jason Boucher of Freewheel bike shop in Minneapolis reports that 58 percent of the store's 1994 sales were mountain bikes. An additional 32 percent of sales were crossbikes, which combine some of the features of a regular road bike with those of a mountain bike.

If you're considering the sport, it's smart to rent first. You can find places to rent bikes in most cities, but in some areas of Colorado, you'll find rental bikes on almost every block. I noticed a tremendous increase since the last time I visited two years ago. Most of the bikes, however, are equipped for paved trails and are not suitable for serious trail riding. It took a while to find rental bikes with good suspension and fit.

Good equipment is critical, but it doesn't substitute for skill. Every other time we had tried off-road mountain biking, we were fortunate to have one of our kids as a guide. Most recently, the recommended trail was far more difficult than we had expected. A heavy snowfall and lots of runoff made the path extremely rough. We bounced over roots and rocks with no relief in sight. Within a couple of hundred feet we needed to dismount and ford a rushing stream.

That's when age and wisdom prevailed. Just a day earlier we had seen two downed riders in need of medical assistance. We decided to head for the paved trails. I'd still choose a mountain trail any day, for unsurpassed beauty and a great feeling of accomplishment. But we also knew our limitations, and the paved trail led to town and a rootbeer float.

# *Marathon Pain Replaced by Boston Fever*

I ADMIT IT. I'VE CAUGHT BOSTON MARATHON FEVER. FOR me and many other amateur athletes, 1996 is not the year of the Olympics, its the year of the 100th Boston Marathon.

I ran my last Boston in 1987. When I started running Boston in 1977, there were only about two hundred women entrants. The people who lined the course were a knowledge-able bunch; I was amazed that they would call my name to encourage me on. The biggest rush of all came at the Wellesley Hills, as we ran the fairly narrow gauntlet formed by the women of Wellesley College. I usually ran my fastest mile of the whole race through that stretch.

After running Boston almost yearly, my spouse and I cut back on our running. In 1987, our daughter, a junior at nearby Smith College, convinced us to visit her and run again. We trained, but not with our earlier dedication. At the starting line, we vowed to be sensible. Yet we felt strong early on and were seduced by the crowds and memories of fast times.

It was a long, hard race. I remembered the last slightly downhill mile could be awful. It was. One reason I haven't done a marthon since is the clear memory of pain.

Yet 1996 has been on our minds. Could we qualify again and run another Boston? Since Hap and I have run all of our Boston Marathons together, his recent knee surgery and five-month layoff tempered our thoughts of 1996. My own running was at a pleasurable, twenty-five-miles-per-week level. The longest run I had done for years was ten miles.

When I checked, I found that the qualifying time for my age group at Boston is 4:05, more than an hour slower than many I ran in the past. It looks possible.

Obviously, I'm not alone in dreaming of Boston in 1996. The Twin Cities Marathon field filled on August 24, 1995, the earliest date on record. Jessica Larsen, administrative staff member for the marathon, was still trying to convince callers that they were too late. "Thankfully, I think the word is finally out that we're really full," she said.

Those who missed the deadline are upset because they know TCM is a great race to use to try to qualify for Boston. It has a well-deserved reputation as one of the best races in the country. It's well managed and the encouragement from the thousands of volunteers and spectators who line the route helps make fast times possible.

The Twin Cities Marathon has shown steady growth since 1991. Its earliest ancestor, the Land of Lakes Marathon, was created by the Minnesota Distance Running Association in 1963. Spectators outnumbered runners that year. Of the five male participants, three crossed the finish line.

Marathon running seemed to reach its peak in the 1980s. The first TCM in 1982 attracted forty-five hundred entrants, which was a record for a first-time race. In 1983, 7,416 registered, although only 4,784 finished. The percentage of women runners has increased over the years, from a low of just under 14 percent in 1982 to 29 percent registered in this year's field.

I'm almost scared to admit I'm one of them. Now what I need is no injuries and some good miles in the weeks that remain.

**Judy Mahle Lutter** is a writer, researcher and speaker who has won numerous awards in the health and fitness arena. She is president of Melpomene Institute, America's only organization devoted to health issues affecting physically active women.

# Melp●mene
mel•POM•uh•nee INSTITUTE

*Founded in 1981, Melpomene Institute for Women's Health Research helps women and girls of all ages link physical activity and health through research, publication and education.*

## You'll Benefit from Joining Melpomene

When you become a member of Melpomene Institute, you become part of an active, caring organization that offers you a number of important benefits. These include a subscription to the *Melpomene Journal,* an authoritative and practical source of new research information, updates and general interest articles; discounts on Melpomene publications, events, videos and gift items; and free use of the Resource Center, which holds more than 4,000 articles and research studies. Membership cost: $32/year.

## Melpomene's Newest Offerings

• **"Heroes: Growing Up Female and Strong"**

This video focuses on the link between self-esteem and physical activity for adolescent girls. Video and Curriculum Materials, $24.95. Video only, $19.95.

• ***Breast Cancer: A Handbook***

This 122-page, spiral-bound book is a companion for a woman, her family and friends while she gathers information, learns about her options and makes decisions about her treatment and self-care as a cancer patient. The handbook is complete, concise and handy. By Linda Brown Harris. $8.95.

• ***The Bodywise Woman***

This 304-page paperback, by the staff and researchers of Melpomene Institute, is filled with reliable information about physical activity and women's health. $13.95.

*For information about membership or products, please contact:*

**Melpomene Institute**
1010 University Avenue
St. Paul, Minnesota 55104
Phone: (612) 642-1951
Fax: (612) 642-1871
E-mail: melpomen@skypoint.com
Web site: www.melpomene.org/